TAO FOR NOW

TAO FOR NOW

Wisdom of the Watercourse

ALAN WATTS

Edited by

Mark Watts and
Brian Wheeler, PhD

www.AlanWatts.org / www.AlanWatts.com

First Printing, 2023

Library of Congress Cataloging-in-Publication Data
Watts, Alan Wilson, 1915–1973, author.
Tao for Now: Wisdom of the Watercourse / Alan Watts.

ISBN-13: 978-1-960583-90-1 (print)
ISBN-13: 978-1-960583-91-8 (e-book)

Editors: Mark Watts; Brian Wheeler, PhD
Cover and Book Design: Darrin Drda
Cover Art: Logan Dennison

Waterside Productions
2055 Oxford Ave
Cardiff, CA 92007
www.waterside.com

Contents

Dedicated to Henry "Sandy" Jacobs,
Alan's close friend, and a playful audio
pioneer who first introduced Alan to
making field recordings.

Editor's Preface

As one of the most eloquent and captivating orators of the twentieth century, Alan Watts (1915–1973) left behind a vast body of work, one which has touched and transformed the hearts, minds, and souls of millions—both in his time and today. Featuring hundreds of recorded seminars and lectures, over twenty books, several dozen mainstream and academic articles, and more than forty posthumous books of his edited lectures, one thing is certain: through and through, Watts' charismatic and sage insight offers timeless wisdom that is vitally needed today. Amongst his legacy of creative works lies one critical outlier, a manuscript left unfinished when he left this world—*Tao: The Watercourse Way*.

The story of this book, *TAO for NOW: Wisdom of the Watercourse*, begins where Watts' final writing project left off. According to Al Chungliang Huang, who was a close friend and colleague, Watts envisioned that *Tao: The Watercourse Way*—particularly its last two chapters—would show how the ancient wisdom of Taoism was "medicine for the ills of the West,"[1] principle among them, the illusion of separation. As Watts wrote in the book's preface, Taoism "is of immense importance for our own times when ... we are realizing that our efforts to rule nature by technical force and 'straighten it out' may have the most disastrous results."[2] Alternatively, he went on to suggest that just as the gamble of trusting others is necessary for a healthy community, "we must also take the risk of trimming our sails to the winds of nature,"[3] living what he described as "the Watercourse Way." That is to say, naturally according with the ineffable Tao (the Way of Nature).

Unfortunately, when Watts passed in his sleep on November 16, 1973, the prospect of chapters six and seven being written died with him. Thus, the culmination of his life's work was destined to be left incomplete. However, rather than the manuscript going unpublished, all fingers pointed to Huang, who had been working closely with Watts on the project, and completed the five-chapter book which was published in 1975—no doubt, far better than anyone else could have. Nevertheless, as Huang recounted in his Foreword:

> After he had finished [chapter five], Alan said to me with a special glint in his eyes, "I have now satisfied myself and my readers in scholarship and intellect. The rest of the book will be all fun and surprises!" Alan had hoped to bring the Tao to his readers the way he practiced and experienced it in everyday living.[3]

While it will undoubtedly remain a mystery how Watts would have filled those final pages, the Alan Watts audio archives hold a multitude of clues and possibilities in its storehouse of over 400 hours of recorded talks. Spanning from 1956 to 1973, the archives feature seminar sessions that Watts gave on retreats, in private homes, and at colleges and growth centers throughout North America, such as the Esalen Institute, as well large hall performances he delivered at churches, Zen centers, public lecture halls, and universities such as Harvard, UC Berkeley, and Columbia. In listening to any of that archived audio at random, one will discover no shortage of fun and surprises. His legendary talks are full of them.

And no one knows their way around Watts' audio legacy better than Mark Watts, Alan's son, whom I'm deeply honored to be co-editing this book with. Rooted in their shared interest of the psychology of religion, mystical literature, art, filmmaking, and visual language, Mark began recording his father in 1968 at the age of 15, and worked full-time with Alan from 1971 to 1973, after moving to Sausalito, California, to live on his father's legendary ferryboat (the SS Vallejo). In addition to helping with recording, book reviews, assisting with interesting fan mail, and driving his countercultural icon of a father on West Coast tours (as well as to and from the airport as he came and went on lecture tours), Mark played an integral role in assessing scores of legendary talks and seminars that were captured on a state-of-the-art open-reel tape recorder he had been entrusted with some years prior. Additionally, he was responsible for compiling series of recordings, which led to the idea of "courses on cassette," fashioning the equivalent of electronic college programs in a comprehensive catalog. And a year later this led to the father-son-duo co-founding the Electronic University with Alan's friend Henry "Sandy" Jacobs in 1973, shortly before Alan's passing.

With the help of Sandy, Watts' long-time audio archivist, Mark went on to produce and distribute the mail-order Alan Watts school-without-walls program. He also produced LP's featuring audio from his father's video programs, which had been recorded in 1972, and were distributed to radio stations and libraries throughout the United States—all of which helped drive Watts' charismatic, much-needed wisdom deeper into the Western psyche.

While the Electronic University eventually evolved into what is now known as the Alan Watts Organization, Mark has been deeply immersed in tending his father's audio legacy for the past fifty years. In addition to managing a collection of over 400 Alan Watts seminars and lectures, Mark has published dozens of books of his father's transcribed and edited lectures, curated a 200-hour audio collection, produced 120 radio programs, and been involved in scores of creative projects that feature his father's work, spanning the realms of film and TV, music and education. Most recently, he launched an audio streaming platform—play.alanwatts.org—that features archival videos and hundreds of Watts' full-length seminars and lectures. In short, Mark has an unparalleled grasp of the audio archives, and continues finding innovative ways to engage listeners and viewers.

Having worked with Mark closely for the past few years at the Alan Watts Organization, I can attest to the fact that he is more acquainted with the Alan Watts audio archives than anyone I'd met during my doctoral studies of Watts' work. Not surprisingly, he knew just which shelves to turn to for the proverbial needles in the haystack we sought to discover in curating this book. As Mark and I began imagining what *TAO for NOW* wanted to be, he recounted that *Tao: The Watercourse Way* "was really half the book," for his father "never got to the grand conclusion about a more effective way of living. He touches on it, but he doesn't do the wrap-up that was intended." No doubt, that unique outcome will forever remain elusive; although it was with that very intent that the current volume came to life.

Determined to put together the most comprehensive collection of Watts' teachings on Taoism for this book, Mark and I scoured all of the audio that has been made public to date, as well as many of the recordings that have remained in what he calls "the vault" for the past thirty years. In the process, we found an astonishing array of unique Taoism-related material that has not yet seen the light of day. Naturally, my inner Alan Watts scholar was pleasantly stunned, almost giddy, in fact, to discover content that Watts never put into writing himself. And while *TAO for NOW* can by no means fully account for Watts' unwritten "fun and surprises," it surely offers at least a glimpse into the territory left untraversed by his untimely passing. In fact, the book kicks off with a series of talks—Philosophy of the Tao—that Watts gave in 1966, which is being published for the first time here.

Curated from a dozen of Watts' sessions on Taoism, *TAO for NOW* outlines a path of least resistance for the West, presenting a guide to living the principles and practicalities of the Taoist "Watercourse Way," which is vitally needed to navigate today's world. As you take in the wisdom of the pages ahead, I encourage you to do so in the spirit of how Huang recommended one read *Tao: The Watercourse Way*: "Paradoxically, it must not be taken as medicine, an intellectually swallowed 'pill,' but allowed joyously to infuse our total being and so transform our individual lives and through them our society."[4]

As you make your way through *TAO for NOW*, you may notice a bit of overlap in some of the material. This is intentional. (Although, we did edit out content if it felt too verbatim and didn't add to what Watts had already said.) Rather than "straighten out" the audio transcripts so that each key topic was only addressed once, we kept in mind that Watts well understood that important things not only bear repeating, but are best addressed from a variety of angles. As such, you will find that Watts approached the core of this book's substance from a multitude of interrelated perspectives, thus offering novel insight, commentary, interpretation, or revelation on any given topic.

Derived from talks Watts gave between 1966 and 1973 in intimate seminar settings, *TAO for NOW* reflects his easy-going and accessible style, indicative of the way he connected with small audiences. While Watts is no longer with us today, the living spirit of his work breathes in the pages ahead. There you will discover not only Watts' explication of Taoism and its fundamental principles, but also insight into embodying the Watercourse Way in your daily life, in everything from meditation and the creative arts to making coffee and washing dishes. Inviting you to break free from societal constructs and egoic conventions, *TAO for NOW* promises to help reveal the clear and spacious nature of your mind, and the timeless, flowing presence of who you truly are.

BRIAN WHEELER, PHD
Inverness, California

PART ONE

Philosophy of the Tao

CHAPTER ONE

PHILOSOPHY OF THE TAO 1

The subject of these sessions is going to be the ancient Chinese philosophy called *Taoism*. In ancient China, there were two predominant philosophies, dating apparently from more or less the same period of history—although scholars dispute this to some extent. Confucius, about whom everybody knows, lived shortly after 600 BCE. The counterpart to Confucius, one called Lao-tzu, is supposed to have been a contemporary of Confucius, but probably lived somewhat later; and he is a somewhat legendary character, about whom we have less historical information.

These two philosophies play with each other in a remarkable way. Confucianism is a social ritual. It is a conception of the order of society—that is to say, a system of social conventions—what you might call a very elaborate and profound form of etiquette. It isn't just a humanistic system, for it has some conception of basic principles of the universe—of harmonious relationship between heaven and earth, and things of that kind. But Confucianism is predominantly concerned with the ordering of family relationships, political relationships, and the language, the ceremonies, and the laws of the land. And this gives me an opportunity to say something about the nature of these social conventions—or we might call them social institutions. Because when we speak of social institutions, we are not simply speaking of things like hospitals, law courts, legislative bodies, and public health systems. Included among social institutions are such things as the clock, the calendar, weights and measures, and above all, language itself.

Confucianism was deeply concerned with what was called *the rectification of names*—that is to say, dictionary making to ensure that people used words in the same way. And we must recognize that a great many things that all of us take for solid realities are, in fact, nothing but social institutions—they are conventions. For example, your idea of yourself—that is to say, your ego image—is not a biological existence; it is a social institution. The characteristics that we associate with men on the one hand, and women on the other, are social institutions. They have very little to do with biology, or even neurology. All sorts of things which we believe to be really "out there" are, as a matter of fact, conventions. For example, you know very well that you cannot tie up a parcel with the equator, because it is an imaginary line. And in exactly the same way, time (clock time) is an imaginary way of dividing and measuring motion. But it so happens that these social institutions become so convenient and so useful that we start to mistake them for the real world.

And that can lead us into an enormous amount of confusion. The same sort of confusion from which you would suffer if, for example, you started eating the menu instead of the dinner. Now, as we civilize ourselves, we can only do so through social institutions. In other words, if we didn't have a calendar, if we didn't have an idea of the directions north, south, east and west—although the Earth being a sphere, there are no such directions—we couldn't get on together. If we didn't have agreements about the nature of language, we couldn't communicate with each other. And if I didn't know about time and space, I couldn't say, "I will agree to meet you at the corner of State and Madison at four o'clock in the afternoon"; and therefore, we could never find each other. But because these institutions are so useful, we come in due course to believe in them, as I said. And above all, we come to believe in ourselves as equivalent with *the role we are playing in life*.

Confucianism was deeply concerned with roles. It addressed questions such as, *What is the proper role of a father? What is the proper role of a mother, of an elder brother, of a younger brother, of an elder sister, of a younger sister?*—and so on all the way around. And you know how it is in our own life: we are all role playing. We play roles according to our occupation in life; we also play roles with respect to our characters. There are certain social kinds of roles, for example, which are acceptable for men to play, and there are certain roles which men ought not to play, according to definition. You very soon are taught by your family, by your friends, to accept yourself as a certain kind of a character. You are told who you are.

For example, you may remember as a child when you went out to play with other children and came home mimicking the mannerisms of some other child, and your parents, being disturbed by this, said, "That's not *you*, Johnny! That's Peter." Because everybody wants to identify you and tell you who you are, and this grows and grows as you go through life—more and more people try to identify you. For example, they say, "Are you a Republican or are you a Democrat? Are you a Presbyterian, an Episcopalian, a Baptist, a Roman Catholic, etc.? Come on now, what are you? Give, tell us." In other words, people persuade you into accepting certain roles, and it's so effective because you eventually come to believe in it all.

One of the funniest things they do to you is that when you're taught who you are as a child, it's practically impossible for you to resist social persuasion. The general effect of what people say to you as a child is utterly irresistible. But they define you as a free and independent agent, and they say, "You are responsible! And we will praise you for what you do well, and blame you for what you do badly." But *you* are responsible—that is to say, you are an independent source of feelings, and thoughts, and actions, and you believe that because you must—there is no way of resisting it. In other words, you are defined as an independent agent because you aren't, and this leads to the most amazing confusions.

I'm not saying that you don't have freedom inherently; I'm saying that the way in which you are defined as free is a way which you cannot resist. And therefore, society goes on to say to you, *you are required and commanded to behave in such a way that will only be acceptable if you do it voluntarily*. That is to say, "Darling, all nice children love their mothers, and of course you ought to love your mother too; but not because I say so, but because you really want to." *Wowwee*! And when you've had that put into you, you live in a state of confusion for the rest of your life—because you are trying to be free as the result of a compulsion which you can't resist. It's completely self-contradictory. So this is one of the problems attached to role playing.

However, when you go on in life, and you realize you're going to wear out, and that your role is wearing a bit thin, you begin to wonder about the human state, and death, and getting sick and decrepit, and you begin to ask questions: *Who am I really? I mean, underneath the role, what is all this? What is a self? What is sensitivity? What is consciousness? What is it to exist? I really don't think I know myself at all.* Now in our culture, at the present time, we don't have very much to offer for people in that condition. It's true we have psychoanalysis, and we have some religions, but when you consider ordinary, standard brand religions in the Western world—and they're now all more or less proclaiming that

God is dead—they don't offer very much except social convention, and rubbing it in, saying *you should be good*.

We've made statistical studies of the subject matter of sermons given all over the United States—on Sunday after Sunday after Sunday—and basically, the vast percentage of them amount to saying to people, "You ought to be good." Everybody knows this, but nobody knows how. "You *must* love"—that's what the preachers are saying. And if history tells us anything, it tells us that preaching doesn't work. Nobody ever listened to it; though they love being scolded. A colorful scolding by a good preacher is a great thrill, but by and large, our standard brand religions, so far as leading one to a real deep and experiential discovery of who and what you really are, and what your situation in this universe is, they don't go very far. You can, of course, read deeply in theology and go quite a long way. But so far as the fare is concerned, which the ordinary person will get in the average church, it's very superficial.

The Chinese, however, devised a philosophy for those who came to this point, and it's called Taoism—which is, as I said, the counterpart to Confucianism. The Chinese character for *Tao* is pronounced "dow." You would think it's pronounced "tao" or "teo," but we've Romanized Chinese in such a way that only those in the know can decide how it's pronounced. We could have spelled it d-o-w, but it's t-a-o. Tao means "the course of nature," "the Way," "the flow of things." And so Taoism is the philosophy of the Way of Nature.

Now, I must start out by saying that Tao cannot be defined. You may think it's rather strange that I am going to talk for a whole weekend about something which nothing can really be said. The book that is basic to Taoism, called the *Tao Te Ching* (that is to say, the *Book of the Way and Its Power*) starts out by saying, "The Tao which can be spoken is not the eternal Tao." And then Lao-tzu goes on to write a book about it, which you may think rather illogical. But this is something very important to understand: that the Tao means that which is absolutely basic. It therefore means, the basic energy of the universe; it means what you are, really—your true self. But in just the same way as you can't bite your own teeth, and in just the same way that you can't look into your own eyes without using a mirror, you cannot define your real self. The hand can't catch hold of itself; the tip of the finger can't touch the tip of the finger; and therefore, I'm sorry, but we cannot make an object out of what we really are.

And that is why any conception of who you really are—that you may entertain—is wrong. So if you think of yourself as *an ego*—that is to say, as a separate center of consciousness and action that is somehow closed up in a bag of skin—this is a false conception. You are *not* that; you are pretending to be that; you are playing at that. But what you really are utterly escapes definition, and therefore, comes under the category of something metaphysical—that is to say, beyond *physis*—beyond nature in the sense of what can be classified, what can be described, what can be put in a box, and said it's either animal, vegetable, or mineral, it's either long or short, black or white, temporal or eternal. Any category you choose to apply is inadequate to this.

So do you mind if we start out with something we can't say anything about at all—but it's fundamental. Look, it's like this: What's the color of your eyes? (I don't mean the iris; I mean the lens.) We say it has no color; it's transparent. But you see, the perception of all colors whatsoever and all shapes whatsoever depends on that transparent lens. So then, you might ask: *What is the nature of consciousness?* No one can say, because consciousness is common to all experiences and there's no way of isolating it. *What is the color of space?* It's the same question. Or when you listen to a phonograph or the radio, everything that you hear—all the human voices, all the noises of different instruments—are all vibrations on a diaphragm. But nowhere does the radio announce that "what you are hearing now is nothing but vibrations on a diaphragm." That is basic to everything heard, and it's taken for granted. So in exactly the same way, the Tao is the basis of everything that goes on, and is taken for granted; it is as necessary to everything that happens as the diaphragm is to the news on the radio, but we ignore it because it's common to everything. The Tao is the basis of every experience; therefore we don't notice it.

You don't notice anything for which you cannot see a limit, and so we can't think about it. But the point is, which is very important to understand, is that you *are* it. And if you discover that—and there is a way of experiencing it which we will go into later—you become, what shall we call it ... *liberated.* You are no longer taken in by the game that you are playing, which is that *"I" am this particular ego that came into this world and will eventually be swallowed up by death—and that will be that.* You see through that game, and you know that is an illusion—however a convincing one. So this is basic: Tao is the course of nature.

Now, the first chapter of Lao-tzu's book starts out with the words, "The Tao which can be spoken is not the eternal Tao." I'm just taking that as a key phrase to give you the first point. Now, what is the second point? That's the beginning of the second chapter of this book, which is attributed to Lao-tzu, and is supposed to have existed from at least 400 BCE. When he starts out the second chapter, he says:

> When all the world knows beauty to be beautiful,
> there is already ugliness;
> When all the world knows goodness to be good,
> there is already evil.
> Thus, "to be" and "not to be" arise mutually.

And mutual arising is an absolutely essential idea for the whole foundation of Chinese thought. The Chinese character for this has two components, one meaning "to arise"—which is originally the figure of a growing plant—and the other means "mutuality," and this is completely crucial to everything I'm going to talk about. Do you see that you can't have a front without a back, that you can't have a top without a bottom, that you can't have the idea of long without the idea of short? You don't have long things before you have short things, or short things before you have long things.

In the same way, you don't have a world in which there are bees without flowers, or flowers without bees. Because, you see, bees and flowers are really the same organism. They look different, just as your head looks very different from your feet, but you don't have human beings who have heads and no feet, or feet and no heads. They go together. Of course, they are rather obviously joined by skin and bone, but bees and flowers float apart. Bees buzz and flowers send out smell and color, but they are in essence the same organism—because they're inseparable—they require each other. So this is the whole idea of *arising together*.

So that in other words, *to be* and *not to be*—the whole notion of *is* and *isn't*—depend on each other. Now, this is contrary to our common sense. We think that *being* is really there and *non-being* isn't. But we are at the same moment afraid that being may end up as non-being because there's so much more non-being than there is being. In other words, there seems to be so much more space than there is solid, and since whatever is solid in the world requires energy, and since energy eventually runs out, we are afraid that it may all end up as nothing—that we may end up as nothing, along with everything else. And we are scared stiff of that because we don't understand that space (or emptiness) and solid are two aspects of one reality—just as front and back, and just as bees and flower go together. They have to go together. You cannot possibly conceive a solid without a surrounding space, and you cannot conceive space without solids occupying it. Because space is, as a matter of fact, nothing but the relationship between solids.

It's like an interval in music: you can't hear melody unless you hear intervals. But the intervals are not there; there are only the tones. The intervals are, in a way, an illusion. However, the hearing of intervals —that is to say, the steps between tones—is absolutely necessary for being able to hear melody. If you don't hear the intervals, you only hear a succession of noises. You are, then, tone deaf (or tune deaf). So you see how important the interval is. And any architect, any artist knows that space is real. We talk about the *functions of space*, astronomers and physicists talk about *properties of space*, *curved space*, so on and so forth. But in the ordinary common sense that most people have, they think space just isn't there. Solids are there. Reality is therefore identified with the solid, with the energy, and unreality with the emptiness.

And there is this, therefore, basic dread which existentialists talk about as "angst"—fundamental anxiety that arises from the fact that the moment you know you exist, you know you could *not* exist; and therefore, all through one's life there is a sort of sword of Damocles hanging over you—that at any minute you might not be—and that's a real scare. Until, however, you come to understand that "To be or not to be?" is not the question. Because *to be* cannot be without *not being*, just as *not being* cannot be without *being*.

And so, for Chinese thought, these two aspects of the world are called the *yang* and the *yin*. The *yang* means the south side of a mountain, which is in the sun; whereas the *yin* means the north side of a mountain, which is in the shade. So they come to mean positive and negative, white and black, male and female. And they are represented in the familiar diagram of an S-curve inside a circle, like two interlocked commas—one black and one white—where each has, as it were, the eye of the comma (or the eye of a fish or tadpole or something) of the opposite color. This *yang-yin* symbolism is sometimes also represented, as in the *Book of Changes* (the *I Ching*), by broken and unbroken lines. And actually, from the symbolism of the *Book of Changes*—which is earlier than any the literature I'm taking about—Leibniz read it in Latin, and from it he figured out binary arithmetic, which is now basic to all computer techniques. Zero and one: all numbers can be represented by zero and one; zero is the *yin* and one is the *yang*. But you see, the whole secret is that the *yin* and the *yang* are inseparable.

When we were little children and everybody taught us "ABC ..." and "1, 2, 3 ..." They didn't teach us the lesson of black and white, of on and off. This belongs in a way, in our culture, to the hushed-up side of things. Now, the lesson of black and white is to realize, for example, that all of your senses are really one sense—a kind of touching. You touch light with your eyes. You touch air vibrations with your eardrums and get sound. Smell is touching gases and dust in the air. Taste is touching the texture of food and things. The touch with the epidermis is perhaps the crudest form of touch, and sight the most subtle.

And do you realize that all sensation whatsoever is a vibration? It goes on and off, over and over—it's a *yoing, yoing, yoing, yoing, yoing, yoing*. But if it goes fast enough, you don't notice the off—you only notice the on. An arc light, for example, is going on and off with terrific speed; so much so that you shouldn't use an arc light in a sawmill, because the on and off can synchronize with the speed of the saw, and a circular saw may appear to be still when it's actually moving. But all things are like that—on and off. Now you can't have a vibration unless it's a wave pattern, where the crest of the wave is on, and the trough of the wave is off. And you can't have a wave which is half a wave. In other words, no wave exists with a crest alone—there must be a trough. A half wave cannot be manifested. Being, you see, is at work—because being is constantly being, non-being, being, non-being—now you see it, now you don't.

So although on and off are different, they are inseparable—like the two poles of a magnet. Now, if you don't realize that—that on-off constitute a unity—then you get scared that off may win. And if you get scared that off may win, then you stop playing the game of black and white (or on and off), and start another game called *on must win*; and then the game degenerates into a fight—it becomes serious—*Wowwee*! The awful awfuls might get the better in the end. They won't. They may appear to, but they won't. But if you don't see that, you get mixed up, and you don't understand the relationship of *yang* and *yin*. So it is the inner connection, or rather the inseparability, of *yang* and *yin*, which is what is meant by *Tao*. That's why Tao cannot be explained.

And the reason, again—if I may put it another way—is that all thinking is classification. It's asking, "Is you *is,* or is you *ain't*? Is it *this*, or is it *that*?" Because after all, if you want to say something is *inside*, it requires an *outside*. You can't have an inside without an outside, or an outside without an inside. Which is it? And you say, "Choose." And of course, Westerners are always choosing.

> Once to every man and nation,
> comes the moment to decide,
> in the strife twixt truth and falsehood,
> for the good or evil side.
> Then it is the brave man chooses,
> while a coward stands aside.

In other words, you must choose. *Which are you?* And we have magnified this into a nightmare, wherein the ultimate consequence and destiny of the cosmos is *Are you saved, or are you damned? Forever.* And what a thrill that decision is.

What people don't understand is that you don't know you belong to the saved group unless there is also a damned group. In every American town there are the "nice people" who live on one side of the tracks, and the "not-so-nice people" who live on the other. In my town of Sausalito, the people who live up on the hill are the nice people; and then there are the people who live on the waterfront, who are Bohemians and Beatniks, and goodness only knows what. Well now, when the nice people on top of the hill meet for their cocktail parties, the main thing that they discuss is how the whole town is deteriorating, and how the awful people are proliferating, and fouling the bay, and so on. And this boosts their collective ego because they know that they are the nice people.

Meanwhile, the Bohemians and Beatniks get together at their parties and play like they are the real in-group, because all those squares and snobbish bourgeoisie who live up on the hill are engaged in a business rat race—doing work which is of no interest in order to buy toy rocket ships, and have wall-to-wall carpets and horribly clean houses. And so the Bohemians and Beatniks boost their collective ego too, by arguing against the people on top of the hill. But what neither side realizes is that they need each other, because if you want to belong to an in-group, you don't know who you are unless you define an out-group.

It is the same with philosophy. There are only two kinds of philosophy in the entire history of philosophical debates. One side is called "prickles" and the other is called "goo." And prickles people are those who like things to be sharp, and clear, and definite. They are the sort of people who become scholars, engineers, and scientists—the type that prefer clear statistics, and discipline, and everything well in order. And they look upon other people—who they think are vague, sloppy, and miasmic, who are romantic, unrealistic, wishful, and so on—and they say, "Ugh! You're just goo." Well, the goo people turn around and say to the prickles people, "Why, you're just bones. You just rattle—you have no skin on you. You know the words, yes, but you don't know the music. You have no finer feelings." And so this goes on forever.

Prickly people want to believe that the ultimate constituents of the material universe are particles. Gooey people prefer to think of it as waves. In classical philosophy, prickly people are nominalists, and gooey people are realists. So it goes—they are always fighting. The thing is, they don't realize that you wouldn't know the standpoint of prickles unless you knew goo as a contrast, and vice versa. Because the real world is gooey prickles and prickly goo—any way you look at it. So you see, that is just the *yang* and the *yin*; the *yang* is prickles and the *yin* is goo—and they are inseparable, but quite different.

And to see the wisdom is to understand the secret conspiracy between the opposites—that you wouldn't know one without the other. That is, as it were, Tweedledum and Tweedledee *agreed* to have a battle; that in other words, under all explicit opposition there is implicit unity. Only, there is no real way of saying it, and in a certain way it should remain implicit and offstage. Don't give the show away. So you might say to me, "Well, why are you talking about this? You're giving the show away, aren't you?" Not really. Because not everybody will believe it. Most people won't. The opposition between life and death, between good and bad, between pleasure and pain is extraordinarily impressive, and though one may point out that it is underneath, a unity, only those with a certain innate intelligence will ever be able to believe it. So one cannot really give the show away. Except, as Jesus said, "To him that hath, shall be given," and, "He who has ears to hear, let him hear."

So this is the point of Taoism. In other words, people involved in practical affairs—in business and family raising—are all upset because *yin* might win, and they really are involved and know they have to do something to survive. Survival is the important thing: you really must go on living. But everyone, as they get older and have raised a family, or whatever they have done, has to eventually get ready for death. And the second half of life is a preparation for death. But that, to Western ears, is a very gloomy enterprise. We pretend death doesn't happen, and we sweep people under the carpet. When you're dying in a hospital, everybody comes around and says, "Oh, you'll soon get better." But the poor dying patient notices there is a hollow look in people's eyes—that they are just consoling—and that's terrible.

When someone is dying in hospital, you ought to come around and say, "Listen, you're going to die. Do you realize you're going to die? It's an occasion for an immense celebration." Because if you accept that you're going to die, you can let go of yourself, and you won't be a nuisance to yourself anymore. And so we should have a champagne party, or we should have sacraments, according to taste. There should be some very special, conscious entry into death—of letting go of oneself—because you only die once, and it should be a very important event. Instead, the morticians come around and pretend that it hasn't happened; they have all sorts of ways of glossing it over. You know that passage in Henry Miller's essay, "The Staff of Life," where he's talking about that dreadful food, and to paraphrase, he says:

> Throw anything down the hatch, and swallow a dozen vitamins. If that doesn't work, see a surgeon. If that doesn't work, try a Hollywood funeral; they are the duckiest, cutest funerals in the world. You can have your beloved one propped up, smoking a cigarette, reading the Bhagavad Gita or something uplifting. A cigarette guaranteed not to rot away before the lips or the

buttocks. O death, where is thy sting. O grave, where thy victory. Jolly wot?

This terrible American way of death does not accept it, pretends it doesn't happen, and doesn't see that death is the most life-giving thing there is. Except the Irish, they can have a wake, but even then, I don't think that in the Western tradition we really get down to seeing how revivifying death is—that, in other words, if in the course of life you die, before you die physically. Now, that means that if you accept the fact that you are completely disintegrating—and there's nothing you can do to hold on to yourself, and nothing you can do to be safe or secure—you come alive.

But everybody imagines they can be secure. You have investments, insurance, regular medical examinations, etc., but this doesn't make the slightest difference. Any minute you can slip on a banana peel or have an automobile accident—because the whole world is falling apart. When you were born, you were kicked off the edge of a precipice, and it's pure illusion to console yourself by clinging on hard to a rock that's falling down with you. There is no way of *not* disintegrating. The whole thing is falling apart, and people have been saying ever since 6,000 BCE that the world is going to the dogs. It is. Life is something that is always falling apart.

But if you get *with it*—in other words, you accept the situation, you flow with it—you come alive. Because you acquire courage, you're not defending yourself all the time. You acquire energy, because you're not all locked up, wondering what's going to happen next. You get the capacity to take risks, and you can't have a free people unless you are willing to take risks—it's all gambling. So this falling apart of everything, which incidentally is what makes it alive—change is life—this is the Tao.

And to flow with the Tao and not fight it—flow with the stream—this is the next great principle of Taoism, which is called *wu-wei*. Remember your principles. The first is *Tao*, which can't be defined. Second is *mutual arising*: the inseparability of the *yang* and the *yin*. And then we get as the third principle, *wu-wei*. In Chinese, *wu* means "negative," "not," and *wei* means "interfering," "clutching," "busyness," "aggression." So the principle whereby a person may come into accord with the course of nature is by *wu-wei*—not clutching. It's sometimes translated "not doing," but in English that is misleading; although sometimes it is the right translation. *Wu-wei* means not acting against the grain of nature—but rather, acting in accordance with it.

The best possible example of *wu-wei* is the art of sailing. You can see that it's much more intelligent to put up a sail than to use oars, because you don't have to work so hard. So a higher form of intelligence would erect a sail—a lower form would just row. But when you sail, you cannot sail directly against the wind. If you want to sail in a direction contrary to the wind, you must tack. So in the same way, if you get caught in an overwhelming current when you're swimming, you can't turn around and swim against it—you will drown in a hurry that way. But what you can do, is you can swim with it and edge out.

So this is the basic philosophy of what is called in Japanese, *judo*, which means "the gentle way." (*Do* is the Japanese way of pronouncing Tao.) And in *judo* you overcome a violent opponent not by direct opposition, but by using the opponent's strength to bring about his own downfall. There's a basic kind of *judo*, slow motion kind of stuff, that is called *ju-no-kata* which exhibits the fundamental ideas of *judo*. And in the first lesson of *ju-no-kata*, which involves two people, the attacker will come straight at the defender with a blow; and the defender, instead of pushing him away, pulls the hand in the direction it's going, and throws the opponent off his balance. So that's the fundamental thing—go with it.

A clever artist, when he is using wood, he studies the grain; he looks at the grain in a block of wood, and asks, *What does it want to be?* There was a competition some years ago, in sculpture, at the Art Institute of Chicago, and it was won by a woman. The competition consisted in each contestant doing something with a cubic foot of plaster of paris. And when this woman looked at it, she said, "It is entirely indifferent: it has no texture; it doesn't want to be anything." So she picked it up and flung it on the floor. Then it was all chipped and full of cracks, and in looking at it again, she decided that it wanted to be something; she saw in those cracks and chips, a form, and she brought out that form and won the competition. So great potters don't simply impose their will on the clay; they feel the texture of the clay, and have the sense that when they throw a pot on the wheel, the pot grows of itself.

Similarly, when you perfect the writing of Chinese characters, you get the sensation that the brush is doing the work. When you skillfully make music, you feel that the music is singing *through you*. There was an occasion once when a great choirmaster in England, Sir Walford Davies, was with the former Archbishop of Canterbury, William Temple, who was a great theologian, and he was training a choir of working men in singing. And he first gave them a hymn to sing that they all knew very well, and because they wanted to impress the Archbishop, they sang it with utmost vigor—and it sounded terrible. So then, he had a professional choir that was there sing the same hymn—so that they could really listen to it.

Now, he said, "I want you to sing it again. But look, one point I must make clear is you *must not try* to sing it. Don't try. All you have to do is to think of the tune and let it sing itself." And then they did very well. So he turned to the Archbishop and said, "That's good theology, isn't it?" And I got the story from the Archbishop, so apparently he approved. So this, too, is the principle of *wu-wei*. Similarly, we have all kinds of common expressions, such as "roll with the punch," and things like that—like Shakespeare saying, "There is a tide in the affairs of men, which, taken at its flood, leads on to fortune." We have an innate folk wisdom which realizes that according with the grain of nature is a fundamental principle.

Whereas the emphasis in the Confucian tradition in China is on interference and keeping things in order to a large extent—and has a certain anxiety about the whole thing—the emphasis of Taoism is to trust in the course of nature, about which I have to tell you two Chinese stories. Both are about farmers and their sons.

One evening the farmer's son came in very, very late from the fields after all the rest of the family, and was late for dinner. And they said to him, "What have you been doing?"

"Oh," he said, "I've been helping the corn to grow."

The next morning, when everybody got up, they found that all the corn was dead. Because what he had done late the night before, was he pulled every new chute of corn up a little, to make it higher.

Another story that is told is about the farmer who lost a horse; it ran away. And all his friends came around and said, "That's too bad."

And he said, "Maybe."

The next day the horse returned, and it brought seven wild horses with it; and they said, "My, that's great!"

And he said, "Maybe."

The next day, his son, in attempting to train one of these horses, was thrown and broke a leg; and everybody came around and said, "Oh, that's too bad."

And he said, "Maybe."

The next day, the conscription officers came around and rejected his son because he had a broken leg. And everybody came to congratulate him, and said, "Isn't that great!?"

And he said, "Maybe."

So you see, this farmer was *with the course of things*, and he knew it goes this way and it goes that way, it goes up and it goes down. Because if it didn't go down, you would never know you were up. And if you try to be permanently up, or always right, it's like trying to arrange everything in this room so that everything is up and nothing is down, or that everything is on the front and there is no back—and that is an impossible state of affairs.

Now, I am going to stop here, because I don't want you to take in too much at once, or to try to. Just to rehearse it, we have discussed essentially three principles. The one that we can't discuss at all—because it's basic to everything—that's the Tao. The next is the principle of mutuality, the interdependence of the opposites—that they are different, but inseparable. And that goes, of course, for you as *self* and the world as *other*. You can't understand what you mean, or sense, or experience as self without the contrasting sense of other. The two arise mutually. That means self and other go together; they are really one, but they look different. And the third principle is *wu-wei*, the art of coming into accord with the course of nature by flowing with it, and not resisting it—not trying, in other words, to make white exclude black, or black exclude white. Now, all that is very simple, but I'm sure it will create lots of questions in your mind.

CHAPTER TWO

PHILOSOPHY OF THE TAO II

What we are discussing in this seminar is the form of Chinese philosophy called Taoism—the philosophy of the Tao, or of the Way of Nature. And this philosophy originates from some period in Chinese history between 600 and 400 BCE, and has had an enormous influence on the course of Chinese culture.

Taoism is attributed to a person by the name of Lao-tzu, which literally translated, means "the old boy," and he was supposed to have been a librarian at the Imperial Court who tired of the sort of snob life of court, and disappeared into the mountains. But before he was allowed to go, the guardian of the gate stopped him and said, "Sir, you are such a wise man that you cannot go off without leaving us some of your wisdom." And so Lao-tzu stayed in the guardhouse and wrote a short pithy book called the *Tao Te Ching*. *Ching*, in Chinese, means a "classic," "book," or "scripture."

The best translation easily available is by Lin Yutang, from the Modern Library, and it's called *The Wisdom of Lao-tzu*. And in this book he also translates whole sections of Chuang-tzu, as a kind of commentary on the earlier text. And Chuang-tzu is the most humorous philosopher that has ever lived. He is full of anecdotes and wonderful illustrations, and has the most amusing way of explaining his own philosophy by parodying it. For example, he has a passage where he says:

> One night I dreamt I was a butterfly, but now I'm confused because now I've woken up and I don't know whether I am a man who dreamt I was a butterfly or whether I'm a butterfly who's dreaming that I'm a man.

And then again, he has an amusing passage where he says:

> When a drunk man falls out of a cart, although he may suffer, he does not die. Because his spirit is in a state of security, he does not suffer from contact with objective existences. If such security may be got from wine, how much more may be obtained from the Tao?

So this is an illustration of what I was talking about last night. And let me review, then, the three principles of this philosophy we covered last night. The first is the Tao itself, and there is no definition for it. It's called "the Way," or "the course of things." It's what everything basically is—what you are. And it can't be defined, and should not be defined—in just the same way that you have no need to bite your own teeth, or to touch the tip of this finger with the tip of this finger, or to look into your own eyes. It's basic to everything—eternal; it's what there is; it's the which for which there is no whicher.

But it would be wrong to translate *Tao* as "God," because the word *God* has associations which this word doesn't have. The word *God* has an association with monarchy, and the Taoist conception of the world—

and the Taoist attitude to politics—is not monarchical; it's strictly democratic. So that's the first principle—Tao is the course of nature.

The second principle is mutual arising. That is to say, that all the great contrasts of life—black and white, positive and negative (or as the Chinese call it, *yang* and *yin*), self and other, long and short—are not, as it were, things in conflict; they are like the north and south poles of a magnet: they go together. And from this arises the fundamental point that you as *self* are one life with everything you call "other"; your inside goes together with everything outside you, and you interdepend—you constitute one life. And it is not that the external world or the environment is conceived as something that determines you, that pushes you around; nor, on the other hand, that you are something that pushes around your environment; you are a single movement—a single life.

However, through a hallucination of upbringing, education, and all kinds of things, we don't feel this. We come to feel ourselves, instead, as separate centers of awareness and action in the middle of a world that is *not* ourselves, and so there develops a hostile attitude, expressed in such phrases as "the conquest of nature." Some people think, for example, of the artist as a person who beats his material into submission, who takes a piece of marble and clobbers it until it does what he wants it to do. But this is not the Chinese conception of man.

Man is seen in Chinese philosophy—in Taoism in particular—as part of nature or one with nature; and therefore, art is a skillful work of nature. The artist cooperates with nature in the same way as the sailor of a sailboat cooperates with the wind. And so this process of cooperation is, in Taoist philosophy, called *wu-wei*. It means, essentially, "not interfering"—not acting in such a way as to go against the grain of things. But on the other hand it doesn't mean passivity; it means acting in accordance with the course, in accordance with the Tao, the Way. And again, sailing is, as I said, the illustration of that.

Now then, as I mentioned, the word *Tao* should not be translated as "God," or be associated with the idea of God as we have it in Jewish, Islamic, and Christian theology. The reason for this is that the model on which the idea of God is based is the model of the great kings of the ancient Near East: the Pharaohs of Egypt, the Shahs or Khans of Persia, and people like Hammurabi of the Chaldean culture—the great law-givers and tyrants. The title of God in, say, the *Old Testament* is the "King of kings," and the "Lord of lords"; and therefore, everybody in relation to God is in the position of being a subject to a king, or perhaps, a child to an authoritarian father. Now of course, this symbolism in sophisticated Christian theology is not intended to be taken literally. A sophisticated Christian is not required to believe that God is the cosmic male parent.

But symbolism has a tremendous force: it influences the way we think, and feel, and behave far more powerfully than abstract ideas. You may consider God to be "necessary being," in the words of Saint Thomas Aquinas, or as that "circle whose center is everywhere and whose circumference is nowhere," to use Saint Bonaventure's phrase, but at the same time you may still say the Our Father prayer, and you may go to church and take part in the courtly rituals where, for example, an important cathedral is called a *basilica*, which is from the Greek *vasiliás* (i.e., a king). And so a basilica is a king's court.

Now, a royal court is a touchy place, where the king sits with his back to the wall, and he has his guardians on either side of him, and everybody who comes in there has to kneel down or prostrate themselves, because they can't start a fight that way. And that shows the king is a very nervous fellow—he doesn't trust anybody. But that, you see, is the pattern of worship in the ancient form of church. Of course, in the

Protestant churches the pattern is not the court of the king; the pattern is a courtroom, and the minister wears the same robes as a judge. It's still a political model though, and that has a great influence on people.

I don't know how you can be citizens of a republic and believe that a republic is the best form of government while also believing in a monarchical order of the universe. It doesn't make any sense. You can't be loyal to the United States and believe in a monarchical theory of the universe—so that requires an adjustment of the whole notion of God.

However, in this Chinese philosophy of the Tao, the Tao is not considered as the boss. There is a passage in the *Tao Te Ching* where Lao-tzu says:

> The great Tao flows everywhere,
> both to the left and to the right,
> It loves the nourishes all things,
> but does not lord it over them.
> And when merits are accomplished,
> it lays no claim to them.

In other words, the attitude of the Tao—supposing we could personify it—would be to bring things into order by letting them go their own way. Now, the *Tao Te Ching* you must remember, is a manual written for the guidance of rulers, and explains how the emperor should conduct himself in order to be a beloved ruler. And the message is *man, get lost; conceal yourself; don't stand above the people; don't make them aware of your weight oppressing them—stand below; behave like water, because water seeks the low level, which men ordinarily avoid.*

So the Taoist ruler would, in our language, be something like the chief of the sanitation department, who is an unknown official, but a very important one. He doesn't ride in great carriages and processions with crowds turning out to cheer. He is a completely humble official who performs an extraordinarily useful task and regards himself as the servant of the people. Hence, you know, one of the titles of the Pope is "the servant of the servants of God." And of course, this was one part of the Gospel where Jesus washes his disciples feet, and explains that he is among them—as one who serves.

But this doesn't somehow fit in with the other imagery of the royal master: "Christ, our royal Master, leads against the foe; forward into battle, see his banners go!" And in Milton's "Paradise Lost," long before there was any trouble with Satan, Milton describes the angelic host of heaven with all their banners and spears and military arrangements. What were they afraid of? Who were they out to attack? The minute you do that, you stir up trouble.

And so, Lao-tzu explains in his book that the moment you have weapons, there's going to be war; the moment you have valuables, there are going to be thieves. And so there's a funny idea underlying Taoism—which you might say is a version of the Golden Age—that once upon a time, everybody followed the Tao naturally; and nobody ever talked about the necessity of virtue—of loving your neighbor, of filial piety, of anything like that—because it was all done naturally. But when it fell apart for some reason or other, then, arose the laws. So he says, "When the great Tao was lost, there came duty to man and right conduct." When there was trouble in the kingdom, one heard of good administrators and loyal ministers because of course, "When everyone in the world knows goodness to be good, there is already evil."

Now, what are we to make of this? Are they meaning literally that once upon a time there was a Golden Age when human beings lived in a natural, happy state, and didn't have governments and taxes and armies? Well, we don't know. It may be harking back to some sort of infancy memory of life in the womb.

One of the key differences between the Chinese concept of the Tao—or you might almost call it the *non-concept*—and the idea of God in the West, is that Western thought feels that the universe, if and to the extent that it is orderly at all, it has to be ruled. The Chinese feel, on the other hand, that things are best ruled by trusting them, which really isn't ruling.

So what you've got, in other words, as between Western mythology and Chinese mythology—and I must say, I'm using the word *myth* to mean not something untrue—but a myth is an image in terms of which people make sense of the world. For example, if you want to explain electricity to a person who doesn't know anything about electricity, you can use water as a symbol of electricity—flowing of water as corresponding in some way to flow of current. Although the parallel isn't exact, it helps. And so in the same way, we use images to make sense of the world.

In the West, we look upon the world as an *artifact*, and it's natural for a child to ask its mother, "How was I made?" That's an absurd question for a Chinese person, because they look upon the world as an *organism*—which is something completely different from an artifact; it's a living body. Now in your body, who's the boss? There's a big argument about this. One school of thought can argue that the stomach is the boss, because after all, it's terribly important to eat; and therefore, the brain is a servant of the stomach—it's a ganglion on the end of a tube.

Basically, human beings are tubes—all organisms are tubes—and these tubes put things in at one end and out the other. And while this maintains the tube, it also wears it out. Well, for some reason or other, this thing is fun—putting stuff in it at one end and letting it out the other—so tubes make more tubes to go on doing it. And then to help these tubes find things to put in at one end and out the other, they grow a ganglion of nerves at one end, and the point of that ganglion is to look around and find things to put in the tube. That's how your brain arrives, you see? That's one school of thought.

Now the other school of thought will say, "Oh, no. That's not it at all! It's the brain that is the main thing, and the stomach exists simply as a servant of the brain—to keep it in power; it's a power supply for the brain." But of course, neither school of thought is right, because they both serve each other. And so with all the organs of the body, no one is boss—they have learned to live together.

And you see, the body isn't composed of bits. Organs in the body are not *parts* in the same way as parts of a machine. You don't create a human body by screwing together a whole lot of organs. When you watch the growth of anything organic—be it a bacterium, or a plant, or a mammal, or even a crystal—you will notice that they are not composed. You see them forming all over at once—getting larger and larger, or clearer and clearer—and not a kind of hammering bits together, at all. Now, that's the growth process. You watch, for example, a fast-motion picture of a rose budding, and you see how the whole thing swells all over, and lets itself out. What is sort of rolled up in simplicity becomes expanded in complexity—now that's an organism.

And so the Chinese look upon the world as an organism; and therefore, it has no boss. And the word *Tao* refers to, not the ruler of the organism, but to the *process* of the organism considered as a whole; and the whole is projected in every one of its parts.

This is perhaps easiest to understand through an image that is not Taoist, but Buddhist. There is this lovely Japanese expression *ji-ji-mu-ge*. *Ji* is a very funny thing in Chinese. First of all, it means "business"—it means "affair" in the same way the French use the word *laissez faire* for business; it means a "thing" or an "event." And *ji-ji-mu-ge* means between any one thing-event and any other thing-event there is no separation, no block. And the image of this is a spider's web, early in the morning covered in dew, where every dewdrop contains the reflections of every other dewdrop. If you look deeply into any dewdrop you will see all the other dewdrops reflected in it; and of course, they will contain the reflections in turn of all the others again, going on forever—so that every part of an organism implies the whole.

The most astounding exemplification of this has recently come out in laser photography. Did you know that you can take a fragment of a photographic negative—just a piece out of it—and with laser beams, you can reconstruct the whole negative from the piece. It's called a *hologram,* and is simply fantastic, because any part of a totality implies the rest. And so the forces of light in a small part of a photographic negative imply the rest of the negative. This is, of course, basic detection—figure out from the piece what the whole was; figure out from the jawbone of a prehistoric skull what the skull looked like. In every part, the whole is implicit, and the whole implies each one of the parts—it's mutual. That's called *ji-ji-mu-ge* in Buddhist philosophy.

So this is all part and parcel of an organic theory of the universe. The Chinese, therefore, look upon the world as a body not composed of parts, but expressing itself in a varied differentiation, so that everybody and every being is something the whole universe is doing—just as every wave is the whole ocean waving, saying, "Yoo-hoo! I'm *here.*" So all of you are the universe saying, "Yoo-hoo! Look at me." And your existence here implies (and is implied by) the most distant galaxies—by everything. So it all is one continuous whole. As Pierre Teilhard de Chardin said, "The only true atom is the universe." (The *atom* means what is undivisible.) "For take any part out of the universe and look at it carefully, and you will see that it is raveled at all its edges"—it's all an interconnection. This goes back to my point: reality is relation.

Let's take the illustration of the four balls, for example, and imagine a universe in which we have only one ball. That's all there is—one ball floating in space. This is a universe in which there is no energy because there's no way of telling that the ball moves. Equally, there's no way of telling whether it's still because movement and stillness are always relative. If there's only one ball, what's it doing? Is it going up, down, or is it just staying there? There's no way of saying either.

Now we bring in a second ball, and suddenly we can see that they get closer together or further apart. But which one is moving? Again, there's no way of telling. One could be still and the other moving; they could both be moving; the other could be still and the other moving. And furthermore, they can only move in a straight line—that's the only possibility. But you see, it took two of them to produce any energy whatsoever.

Next, three balls. Now two of them stay with each other, and another one seems to go away and return. Which is moving though? The two, are they moving away from the one, or is the one moving away from the two? Well, the only way of deciding is by vote. Two constitutes a majority, and if they decide to stay together, then they say, "Well, you're moving away from us," or "We don't like you, we're moving away from you." But if number three stays always the same distance from the two, it licks them by joining them. Nobody can move at all now.

Therefore, to decide which is moving—the one or the two—let's introduce a fourth ball as an umpire. Incidentally, three balls gave us the possibility of moving within a surface, but four introduces a third dimension, and we can move within a solid. Now you might say four takes an objective point of view, and can look from above and outside at the behavior of the other three, but then the next argument is *which of them is the fourth?* All of them can be in a third dimension with respect to the other three; and that's just a very simplified version of astronomy and of the distribution of bodies in space. It's all based on that principle—that existence is relativity. In other words, without relationship there can be no motion; and existence is motion is energy; and pattern implies relationship, and energy is further to be understood in terms of patterned behavior.

So then, it all fits together: everything implies everything else in an organic structure. Now, you might say, "Well, I don't see that because people come and people go, things come and things go, but the universe goes on forever. Are you telling me that if I disappear, the universe is going to disappear with me?" Or put it in another way, "that before there were any living organisms there was no geological reality—no planets, no sun, no stars?" In a way, that's true. When we study the past of the universe, we are saying what it would have been like if there had been someone there to see it. But I will venture a less startling theory: your existence implies the whole universe; the whole universe cannot exist without you. But notice that you are only six feet odd in length. In space, you have a limitation: you don't go on below your feet or above the top of your head. Imagine somebody infinitely long—nobody could see them. If you were married to an infinitely tall woman, you would divorce her on grounds of desertion.

Now, in the same way, you can't be infinitely long in time. Something that doesn't have limits in time has no rhythm to it; and therefore it doesn't exist. To get existence, as I pointed out, you've got to have rhythm and wave motion. It's got to vibrate, and go *yoi-yoi-yoi-yoi-yoi-yoi-yoi-yoi-yoi*—otherwise it isn't there; it's got to go on-off. So you necessarily live a short time—you start, and you stop. But the whole universe depends on your being there at some time—not all the time, but at some time. In other words, all ages—past, present, and to come—depend on you being here now, for so many years. It all hangs on that. You can see it in the case of somebody famous, like Socrates. The fact that Socrates did once exist is a symptom of the possibilities and of the nature of humanity. This is true also of John Doe or Mary Smith. So all the world depends on you, even though you come, and you go, you appear, and you disappear—just as you, in turn, depend on all the world.

CHAPTER THREE

PHILOSOPHY OF THE TAO III

Well now, having then seen the organic nature of the universe, we can go on to discuss what kind of order an organism has. And this is where we move in the direction of studying the influence of Taoism upon art. Strangely enough, the Chinese don't really have any expression to mean the "law of nature"—because they don't think of nature as responding to law.

There was a young man who said, "Damn,
For it certainly seems that I am,
A creature that moves in determinate grooves.
I'm not even a bus, I'm a tram."

And that's the idea of the law of nature—that there are set up principles upon which things must operate. We say things "obey the law of nature"—that a falling stone "obeys the law of gravity." Of course, it does nothing of the kind. Gravity is a way of describing the behavior of falling stones; they're not *obeying* laws. They do this in a regular way, otherwise, they wouldn't be stones unsuspended in free space; it's not a law that they obey.

But in Chinese, our idea of law is represented by the word *tse*. Originally written in the old seal-style writing, the character for *tse* is presumed to be a drawing of a sacrificial cauldron with a knife beside it, because there were certain emperors in very ancient times who had the laws of the country engraved on the sides of sacrificial cauldrons, so that when the people came on ritual occasions to put their sacrifices into the cauldrons, they would read the laws. And so *tse* means what we call "positive law"—what you *must do* or *must not do*. Now, the sages—especially the Taoist sages—at these times reprimanded the emperors and said you should never write the laws down because people will develop a litigious spirit.

The Confucians were interested in the rectification of names—that is to say, in dictionary making—and were always laughed at by the Taoists because the Taoists said that if you want to fix the meaning of words, you have to define the meaning in terms of words. Now, how do you define the meaning of the words that define them? Aren't you always getting into difficulties? And this is the trouble with dictionaries.

Do you know how to play a game called Vish? It's great fun. Supposing you have five players, each one has a copy of the same dictionary (say, *Webster's Collegiate*), and then you have a number of words which are drawn from a hat, and you draw out a word and everybody looks up that word and gets the definition. Then you look up a key word in the definition of that word, and record each word looked up, and then when you get back to the original word, you call out "*Vish!*" (*Vish* means vicious circle.) So the person who calls out Vish first wins the round. And a referee decides whether the winner was honest about it, whether the words used were significant words in the definition of each word that was looked up. Well, that's the nature of dictionaries: a dictionary doesn't really give you any information—unless it has pictures in it—it explains words in terms of words in terms of words. And that's the trouble with *tse* as law.

So the Tao is called, specifically, *wu-tse*, which means "lawless"—it does not operate by that kind of law. Now, this is the only word that could possibly be used in Chinese for our meaning of the law of nature. There is a word in Chinese that is sometimes translated *law*, especially in Buddhism, and that is *fa*, the original meaning of which was probably a "water level"—like what we call a *spirit level*—for seeing whether a thing is horizontal or perpendicular, although some scholars disagree. I prefer to translate this word "method"—the method of Buddhism. Buddhism is not a law. In Buddhism there is no *thou shalt do this* and *thou shalt not do that.* The moral precepts of Buddhism are vows, not laws; they are obligations that you take upon yourself—not rules that you obey.

So when we try to find a word in Chinese that really describes the law of nature—that is to say, the order of nature—we will use the word *li.* This is one of the most fascinating words in the Chinese language, because the original meaning of *li* is "the markings in jade" (you know, the mottled effect in jade). It also means "the grain in wood" and "the fiber in muscle." And this word is sometimes translated—I think mistranslated—"reason" or "principle." The *principle of the universe*—that's not too bad. But I think that Joseph Needham—who is a great British, Chinese scholar—is right in saying that the proper translation for this word *li* is "organic pattern."

Now, here comes the thing: What is the difference between an organic pattern and a mess? This is a crucial question for painters and all artists and sculptors today because they want to get spontaneity into their work. But there are some charlatans who, for example, get a typewriter and melt it, and hit it with a sledgehammer, and then put it on a pedestal and call it a piece of sculpture. One knows in looking at it that it's a mess—but you can't say why. There is no rule for explaining this. And on the other hand, you look at some other work where it's just as spontaneous, and you realize it's not a mess—but you have difficulty in saying why.

Well now, one of the funny things about art is that every state park in the United States, practically, has a place in it where you look out at a view called Inspiration Point, and all the tourists go there and they say, "Oh, it's just like a picture." Why do they say that? It's because it was painters who taught people to look at landscape. Before painters started painting landscape, nobody bothered with it. Painters teach us to see. In a few years from now, ordinary people will walk by an old wooden fence covered in bird droppings and slop of paint, and they will turn and say, "Oh, it's just like a picture"—because Jackson Pollock taught them to see a fence. But as it is now, when an ordinary square or philistine goes into an art gallery and looks at an abstract, he says, "That's not what I call a picture. What's it *of*? My child could do as well!" And I say to such people—and sometimes this really bugs them—"That's not a painting; that's a colored photograph."

"Say what?"

"Yes, it's a colored photograph."

"Well, what's it of?"

"Well, take a good look. I don't know what it's of. It may be a microscope slide or something."

And this really alarms people. Or else I'll say, "Look, this never was intended to be a picture of anything. It's just a creation, not a picture. It's a painting, something that an artist did—just like the tree does a leaf." Because, here's the thing. Supposing I paint a cloud—why paint clouds? What are clouds representations of? A cloud doesn't represent anything. A cloud *is* a cloud; it's not a picture. But you see, the artist sees the cloud as so beautiful that they do it the compliment of painting it. If I paint an abstract painting, I am making my own cloud.

But here's the question: Why is it that you never see badly formed clouds? Clouds never make aesthetic mistakes. Patterns in sea foam never make aesthetic mistakes. Would anybody criticize the stars for being improperly arranged? Do you praise the peaks for being high or blame valleys for being deep? No, and this is the fascinating thing, because all nature is in accord with *li*. And that's how you recognize a certain quality of order that is not symmetrical order—that you can't fit into any mechanical pattern—but you know it's not a mess. Now, to understand this you must not try to explain it—there is no way of explaining it. If you could explain *li* you would destroy it. In exactly the same way, if you had a teaching method that would infallibly produce great painters, you would destroy the art of painting. Because the whole point of an art, or of an artist, is a surprise. When we marvel at an artist, and say, "How did you do it?" and they have to say, in the end, "Well, I don't know."

So Chuang-tzu tells the story of the wheel-maker who has to get a wheel just exactly right, so that it won't wobble on the axle, but at the same time it won't stick on it. And he says, "I have been doing this for seventy years, and I don't know how I do it; and therefore, I am still working and cannot pass on the craft to my son." In the same way, there's a story of a butcher who is so skillful with the knife that when he cuts up meat, he always gets the edge of the knife exactly through the interstices between the bones, and so he has had this knife for seventeen years, and it has never been sharpened. Because that which is infinitely thin can go through the place where there is no aperture—that's the way Chuang-tzu explains it.

And there are many, many passages in Taoist literature on these skills, and they all have to do with the comprehension of *li*. And this is a thing that you have to have in your bones. You know, when you're cooking, people want a recipe book that tells you exactly how much salt, spice, how long to bake it, etc. But have you ever tried to boil eggs from a recipe? Boiling an egg is a weird thing because it depends on so many variables: how hot your stove is, how hot or cold the egg was when you started, whether it was a real farm egg or a pseudo egg—because now days we are getting pseudo eggs—and the shells are made of nothing. It depends on all sorts of things. What is the difference between simmering and boiling? When does water actually begin to boil? When does it start to simmer? Everybody has a slightly different idea about this. But one of the best egg boilers I know never watches a clock. She simply puts the egg in, and when she feels it's ready, she brings it out and it's perfect. Some people say so many Hail Marys and then bring it out, or something like that. All this is subtle, so you have to cook by taste and feel.

It's the same way with such skills as golf, archery, and shooting. There's a feel for it, and this feel can never be sufficiently and accurately rendered in words, and if it could, it would not be it. I remember a Japanese artist, Saburo Hasegawa, and he was teaching the history of Far Eastern art, and all these students would crowd around him at the dinner table and try to get him to say exactly what he meant by, say, the Japanese term *sabi*. *Sabi* means, well, it's like how you feel when you see a crow all huddled up by himself on a tree branch, on a cold autumn evening. It's not that the crow is miserable; he's alone, quiet. And then the student would say, "But what is the precise difference between *sabi* and *wabi*, now? Does it really mean *solitary*?" Suddenly this man said, "What's the matter with you! Can't you feel?"

And this is so much the case with our students. Because you see, all of us, insofar as we are educated for our careers, are brought up to be bankers, clerks, insurance salesman, and bureaucrats. That is to say, our education is one-sidedly literate. We value only three kinds of intelligence: *mnemonic* (good memory), *computational* (can you figure), and *verbal* (are you articulate?). And therefore, we produce an absolute minimum of people who are sophisticated in any kind of physical competence. Think of this: in high school, people are encouraged to learn competence in physical skills only when they are sort of apt to be dropouts. They're not expected to go on to college, because they don't have very much brilliance by these measures of intellect, and so regretfully, they are given courses in carpentry or metalwork.

But in the things above all in which we need physical competence, what are they? Cooking, furniture-making, house-making, clothes-making, and love-making. In all these things we are unbelievably inept because physical competence is supposed to be something for peasants. So it's more and more difficult to buy anything—clothes or whatnot—that is any good at all. You have to go out of the country for it, and get it from peasants. We are not good at these things partly because we are thinking about everything in words. We have manuals of instruction and do-it-yourself kits. Take the following steps: one, two, three, four, five. Maybe if you've got some gift for it, you can use it. But you see that whole *feel for things* is the most important kind of intelligence that a human being can have—and that is *li* intelligence, which cannot be taught. You have to get it by osmosis, or somehow find it out for yourself.

A Zen story is told of a professional thief who wanted to teach his son the art of robbery. So he took him on a robbery with him one night, and made him get inside a big chest, he slammed down the lid, and left him. Then suddenly he called out, "Thief! Thief! Thief!"—and ran away. Here was the son in the box, who realized that everybody was alarmed in the house, and they were all looking for him; and he knew there was just one chance, so he scrambled out of the box, rushed into the garden, grabbed a rock and threw it down the well, and hid. And everybody thought, "Oh, the thief ran out and jumped in the well, and committed suicide!" because he knew he would be executed, if caught. Then when they went away, he went home, and the father said, "Good. You learned the art."

Now, what does this further lead to? How could the boy be so ingenious as to know that? I mean, wouldn't he have to be taught? Wouldn't he have to have seen before or heard some story of some other burglar who had used this trick? This is what we call in modern psychology "the problem of learning theory." *How do we learn? How do we develop ingenuity?* Now, there's a lot of nonsense about this. Because if you assume that everything is learned from a former example, then knowledge can be nothing but an ever-progressing repetition of itself—an ever-continuing regurgitation of old information. But obviously it isn't. People think up new things, new ways of doing it.

How do they do it? The answer is that your own brain is incredibly ingenious—much more ingenious than the conscious attention powers give it credit for. And so when you want to solve a problem, you have to trust your brain: give the problem to your brain. As we say sometimes, "Sleep on it"—because this marvelous computer that you have in your skull is much smarter than you are. (And when I say, "*you* are," I mean, if you define yourself simply in terms of your conscious attention.) So all these skills where, for example, the Zen master responds completely appropriately to an unexpected situation, it's because he's been trained to trust his own brain, and let the brain make the decision for him—instead of his trying to make the decision—because in every respect, the brain has the character of *li*.

Now, you may say again, it's stupid to trust your own brain. Do you mean to say that I'm going to do the first thing that comes into my head all the time? Later on you are because that's what you do anyway. But you've got to cultivate this capacity. Actually, you always do the first thing that comes into your head. Supposing you have got some important decision to make, and you think about it, you write down pro things and con things, and then you think, "Well, I think I ought to get some more information about the situation." So you get some more information. Well, now the time is getting short, and you've got to decide anyhow; there isn't time to get any more information, and so you have to say—for completely arbitrary reasons—"Okay, let's decide," and you practically come down to flipping a coin. Now, that's not making a rational decision. That's acting on the spur of the moment, actually—only you go through the pretense that you haven't acted on the spur of the moment, and that you've thought about it very carefully.

Of course, the Chinese have a very clever method of flipping a coin. An ordinary coin only has two sides, but they have an eight-sided one which can give 64 solutions when you toss it. It's called the *Book of Changes* (the *I Ching*), which I'm not going into now. But the point is, that if you can admit the possibility of trusting your own brain, you can gradually acquire confidence. For example, I'm an experienced public speaker, and I don't think up in advance what I'm going to say. I don't think before I talk. I just talk, and think as I talk. Or let's take comedians. When they get on the stage, they can make people laugh and make jokes from completely unpredictable situations. They don't have a routine that they've planned. A good comedian can just simply walk onto the stage, and everybody starts laughing; they want to laugh, they cooperate with him. And he can gag under any circumstances and make it funny. This is because he's got what we call *self-confidence*, and you simply have to have this. If you start doubting and wobbling, then you're not trusting your own innate intelligence; and that innate intelligence is, of course then, the *li* of the brain.

Well, you say, "Oh, dear me. I don't know whether I dare. I just, I can't stick my neck out like that." Now I can encourage you, and say, "Don't you realize that you are, in fact, doing this all the time?" That just as I showed you, you make your most important decisions mainly because you're sick to death of thinking it out, and you have to decide to do something. That's really what it comes to. So in the same way, really and truly deep down, you are living quite spontaneously. And if you have your eyes really open to see people, you will see that they are all as faultless as the markings in jade or lines in marble. It's only because you have fixed ideas of what a face *ought to look like* that you say someone is beautiful and someone else is ugly. But if your eyes are open, everybody is beautiful—and in fact, quite fantastic—gods and goddesses sitting around.

Only to see this, you have to slow down, and get in what I will call *the mood of eternity*. This afternoon sitting around here is, after all, the point, isn't it? You haven't come to hear me in order to get something, have you? Or are you just here to *be here*? I mean, where else would you be? See, get rid of purpose. There's nothing coming; there's no future; there never will be any future—it's always now. And if you keep looking ahead for something out of the future, nothing is going to happen—except perpetual frustration and disappointment.

You know, there are punishments for people who do this. For example, there's a special art to making coffee, and it can't be hurried. The proper way to make coffee is to put as many cups of cold water as you need in a saucepan and an equivalent number of heaping tablespoons of coffee on top of the cold water. Turn on the gas and watch it. Just before it boils, turn out the gas or take it off the electric ring, stir it, and leave it for a little while. It will clear itself and will be the best coffee imaginable. The people who don't have the patience to do that have instant coffee, which is a punishment for being in a hurry.

So in the same way, anything done like that is an attempt to get to the future—to hurry it up! And what you end up with is just kind of a mouthful of papier-mâché and plaster of paris—that's all you ever get—and everything is beginning to be made of it. I've thought of marketing a special substance which is made of papier-mâché, plaster of paris, and artificial flavoring that could be sold as a universal solvent for everything: building houses, cooking, etc.

So you see, there isn't any future, and as soon as you discover that, you can *be*. Otherwise, the only thing you can be, is *in a hurry*. In other words, as you listen to me, don't try to understand me—don't try to get anything out of me. Listen to the sound of the words just in the same way as you look at the shapes of clouds, and then you'll get what I'm saying. If you try to make sense of it, you won't.

PART TWO

Being in the Way

CHAPTER FOUR

BEING IN THE WAY I

One of the first things which everybody should understand is that every creature in the universe, that is in any way sensitive and in any manner of speaking conscious, regards itself as a human being. That is to say, it knows and is aware of a hierarchy of beings above it and a hierarchy of beings below it. If you take such a tiny creature as a fruit fly—which lives only a few days—it is aware of all sorts of weird little animals and objects and spores floating in the atmosphere which we don't even notice unless we've got a microscope around, and very few people have. It criticizes them as being inferior animals, and all that sort of thing, whereas human beings are things that it doesn't comprehend; they are as much outside its intellect as a quasar is outside ours. And we see these far-off objects floating in the heavens, and we have only the vaguest idea of what they may be. Actually, we may all be some kind of atoms in another dimension, with all these galaxies being the constituent elements. Who knows?

But there is, I think, a fundamental principle that everybody must understand in order to know the meaning of the Tao—or the Chinese sense of the course of nature—and that is the principle of relativity. Relativity is absolutely fundamental to an understanding of Taoist philosophy. That is to say, that wherever you are, and whoever you are, and whatever you are, you're in the middle. And so, just in the same way as when you stand, for example, on the deck of a ship and you can see a horizon all around you to exactly the same distance, you're in the center of a circle because your senses extend in all directions, and therefore, give you the impression of being in the middle. Now everything in the world feels like that; and also, it has its own kind, which look natural to it. You see, spiders, and hydras, and sea urchins, and so on don't look very natural to us. We say, "Well, I wouldn't want to look like *that*!" But they say, when they see us, "Well, what kind of an awful thing is *that*? And what a lot of nonsense it does."

But now, here is a very strange thing: Every creature, therefore, which feels that it is human, and which knows that it's there—in the same way as you know you're here—experiences a sensation of a certain tension which constitutes the feeling of *I-ness*, of *there-ness*, of *being here*. Because, after all, every creature is a particular form; everything is individual. Not only "you" as a total organism standing here, but all the component cells of your body; each one of them has some sort of a feeling of its own; it is individual. You can look at it in a microscope at the right level of magnification and you can see that thing *there*, with its own little life. And if you examine the stream of your blood, you will find it full of all kinds of organisms that are having all sorts of conspiracies, and games, and plots, and eating each other, and doing these things like we do. Only, we must realize that we wouldn't be healthy as a total organism unless there were all these wars, fights, plots, and politics going on between the various cells in our blood.

But from their point of view, they feel a little bit put out. And we are in the same situation, because very slowly, the human beings on the surface of the planet are realizing themselves into a total planetary organism with an electronic nervous system. In science fiction, which was published around about the 1920s, it was always expected that future human beings would have enormous heads, because they would have very big brains and they would be very wise. It didn't work that way. What's happening instead is that the human race is building a brain outside its body—that is to say, an interlocking electronic network of telephonic, television, radionic communications, which is rapidly being interlocked with computers so that you will, within a few years, be able to plug your own brain into a computer. You will have a little gadget behind the ear, that will look slightly like a hearing aid, and that will be integrated with your brain in such a way that you can plug-in.

That will only be an intermediate stage, because in exactly the same way as when we thought that all communications by electricity had to go through wires, and then we got rid of the wires and got radio and television, we will eventually get rid of telephones, radio, and television and will communicate by some entirely new method that is, at present, called ESP. But that will mean that absolutely nobody has a private life anymore, and you will have no defenses—everybody else will see right through you. Some people will protest, and say, "Well, this is terrible; there's no privacy anymore. That means there's no 'me.'" Well, that's what has happened to your own cells and your own neurons, and they objected at some time in the course of evolution: "We're getting our private life taken away! We're being organized into a body."

And we are doing the same thing, only we have to try and see if we can be clever about it. That is to say, to do two things at once: to have this tremendous openness to each other—whereby I don't care if you read my thoughts, and you don't care if I read yours—but at the same time, nevertheless, each one of us retains a peculiar individuality, almost in the same way as nothing could be more unlike a stomach than a heart, despite the fact that it is an organism functioning all together. So then the problem is, as I said, is that for each individual which is a separate thing, instead of using the word *separate*, I would rather use the word *distinct*. Separate as I use the word means disjointed, cut off from; but distinct means a feature of something, where an absolutely distinguishable pattern is part of a larger pattern of a whole. And something can be distinct without being separate, in just the same way as back and front can be very different, and yet inseparable. So then, there is this sensation of practically every living being of constituting a center of tension and of resistance, that is to say, of being a little bit blocked—or shall I say, of *being in the way*—being in one's own way.

Imagine the opposite. Let us suppose, for example, that you got up in the morning with a feeling of total transparency—there's no resistance in your organism to the external world. You just float through it; you are part of it, it's part of you. And just in the same way, for example, that when you see—if you see well—you are not aware of your eyes. But if there's something wrong with your eyes, and you see spots in front of you, then you are looking *at your eyes*, and your eyes are getting in your own way. So the Taoist sage Chuang-tzu says, that when clothes fit well, you are not aware of them. When your girdle or belt fits properly, you are not aware of it. Good shoes, you're unconscious of. And so in exactly the same way, the perfect form of man is unaware of himself—because he does not get in his own way. He is, in this sense, completely transparent.

Now you may be thinking that I'm trying to sell you a bill of goods, that I'm going to teach you some technique so that you can feel perfectly transparent, and that this is the proper way to feel—this is the way you *ought* to feel. Now, it's not that simple. The point is, to begin with, you may in a really rather natural way feel alone, and feel a little bit vulnerable—that you've got a soft skin, a weak heart, and you've got all those ills that the human body is heir to going on inside you. Let's begin with that, and the fact that we hurt a bit, and through hurting a bit we know we're here. And this is part of the whole meaning of penances, and all sorts of trials that people go through, and all kinds of adventures, and all sorts of very uncomfortable massage experiences, and so on. As a result of this, it becomes quite apparent that you do truly exist—that you are *there*. You are a kind of an obstacle to the flow of life, and as life impinges upon you, *Wham-o!* But you rebound, and you hurt a bit, and so you are there.

Now then, although people cultivate this, they say in general that they would rather it not be that way; we would like to forget ourselves. And so ever so many people say, "Well, I want somebody to lose myself in; I want something to belong to; I want to join a religion where I can sort of feel that I take part, that I mean something," Or, "I go to the movies to forget myself; I read a mystery story to forget myself; I get drunk to forget myself." Because the peculiar quality of the drug called alcohol is that it turns you off. It makes you increasingly insensitive to pain, and to being—so that you can get a certain vague sense, a rather misty sense, of floating. But as things stand, one ordinarily doesn't feel that way, and therefore takes something like that in order to disappear, in order to feel less this sensation of resisting the world.

Did you know that if you study your body in its dynamics, you will find that you are fighting all the time? Most people are, some aren't. But most people are fighting the external world all the time. My friend Charlotte Selver often tries an experiment where she makes a person lie down on the floor and says to them, "Now look, the floor is solid, and it will hold you up. You don't have to do anything to stay where you are. Just lie on the floor." Then she looks at the person, or may touch them slightly, and says, "Do you realize you are making all sorts of efforts to hold yourself together?" Because you are basically afraid that if you don't do that, you will just go *blaaaahhh*—and disappear into a kind of formless goo all over the floor. But you won't! Your skin, bones, muscle tonus, and everything is all there naturally, and it will hold you together. There's nothing to worry about, and all you have to do is lie on the floor; you don't have to make any special efforts to stay together.

But many people are afraid that they will fall apart, or somehow disintegrate if they don't make efforts to hold themselves together, or else that they will be disintegrated by some outside agency if they are not constantly on the alert all around to protect themselves. Now, I'm not a preacher—that's the most important thing to understand about me. I'm not saying you shouldn't do that, but I am inviting you to become immensely aware of the fact that if you do that at all, that *you* do it. And that you have, therefore, this sense of being alone, of being a particular separate form that is unlike any other form on Earth, that is just you—and you concentrate on that. After all, for many people, they define this as their problem, so you ought to be able to feel it without the slightest difficulty. It isn't as if I were asking you to feel some transcendental sensation or something of that kind. This is just a very ordinary sense of being you, and of being alone.

Now, as you focus on that sensation of distinctness—we'll even call this one *separateness*—because we have been brought up to feel separate, we have been brought up to feel actually dis-joined from the external world; although that is pure mythology, and doesn't exist at all. You are as much part of the external world as a whirlpool is part of a stream, but we're brought up to not notice that. And if you've been brought up that way, and you don't notice that you are as much part of the world as a whirlpool is of a stream, you feel this intense separateness.

And the thing to do with all feelings that you don't like is to experience them as deeply as possible, and go into the innermost depths of loneliness—indeed, let us say, the innermost depths of selfishness. Are you selfish? You know, lots of people try to pretend they are not, and say, "Well, I try not to be, but I guess I don't succeed all the time." And so Krishnamurti, you may know, is a very devil because he always roots it out. He shows all the people who are very good, and have the highest ideals, and who are doing everything, that they are really doing it for the same sort of motivation as other people who are robbing banks. Only they're giving it a name so as to conceal it better—that's culture.

Culture is a way of more cleverly concealing the fact that you have to eat. Like the Queen of Spain, who in the days of the 1860s, floated into the room with these enormous skirts, and was sort of coming on like she was an angel. And when they were first invented, somebody gave her a present of beautiful silk stockings—a dozen pairs—and sent them to the Queen. And Her Majesty's chamberlain replied with a letter returning the stockings and saying, "Her Majesty the Queen of Spain does not *have* legs." But she managed to float along just the same because she's an angel.

So you see, all kinds of high culture use subtle ways of concealing and pretending that we do without the things that the lower classes do—whether of humans or of animals. We pretend that we don't. It's like, you don't go around crudely taking a bull and banging it on the head with a mallet, or sticking a knife through it and tearing it apart and eating it. All that's done somewhere off in the stockyard, and it comes to us in the butcher shop as a completely neutral looking thing called "a steak." The steak has absolutely nothing to do with a cow—it's something wrapped up and packaged. Nobody who picked up a steak, and tested it, would think: "It's a poor cow." It doesn't even look like a cow! Doesn't remind you of one in any way. So that's culture, however much you mask it under lofty ideals.

I mean, the most religious people in the world, even the greatest saints, are the most nefarious rascals. I've known lots of them. So when anybody is frighteningly holy, you know that that guy is just playing an extremely far-out game, because he has put so many layers and so many wiggles between what he is outwardly doing, and his inward, irreducible rascality—that he is a very cultured being indeed, and is playing a very complicated game.

In Hebrew theology, incidentally, it is admitted quite frankly that there is a thing called the *yetzer ha-ra*. And in the beginning of time, when God created Adam, he implanted in him the *yetzer ha-ra*, which means "the wayward spirit." He put something funny in man so that man would be a little odd, and it was a result of the *yetzer ha-ra* that Adam was tempted by Eve—who was tempted by the serpent—to eat that famous fruit. But the Hebrew believes that everything that God created is good, including the *yetzer ha-ra*.

Because if it had not been for the *yetzer ha-ra*, nothing would have ever happened. Everybody would have obeyed God, and God would have said, "Well, this is kind of a bore." And so now, you can't just come up to someone and say, "Disobey me." Because if they do, they're obeying you. That's a double-bind, to say to somebody, "Disobey me." But God was much more subtle than that. He didn't tell Adam to disobey him; he told him to obey. But subtly, he put the *yetzer ha-ra* in, so that God would say, "Well, I'm not responsible"—this thing is going to happen of its own—because what everybody wants is something to happen on its own. In other words, something comes back, and I'm not quite sure what it's going to do. And it's to the degree that I encounter something like that that I know it's alive—and everybody wants that. Because, you see, that is the sensation of being *you*—this curious, lonely center of awkward sensitivity, subject to the most peculiar feelings, and pains, anxieties, and all that sort of thing—and all that is an essential prerequisite for feeling *something else*. These two experiences go together.

Now you may want to be omnipotent, and live in a universe where nothing happens except exactly what you will to happen. In other words, you say, "I would like to be God"—if you think that's the way God is—"and everything is, therefore, totally under my control; everything is absolutely transparent to my intelligence. I have no problems." And there are a lot of people coming on like they think they've attained this state, people like Meher Baba, who says he's in charge of the universe, and knows everything, understands everything, and so on and so forth. Well, that's a lot of bunk. Nobody wants to be in that position because there wouldn't be anything to it. Because once everything is under your central control, nothing is happening—it's a bore, from beginning to end. So for anyone (or any being whatsoever) who has a sense of centrality—who has a sense of selfhood, who has a sense of identity—that sense of identity is inseparable from something else going on, something defined as *not* being me, as *not* being under my control, and that may jump at any time. It might even eat me.

So what I want you first of all to understand, is that these two sensations—of being the lonely, central, sensitive, vulnerable self, and of living in the midst of a world that feels "other," that is not under your control—I want to try and show you that these two sensations are really one sensation. Or rather, two aspects of one sensation. You couldn't have the one experience without the other experience. Now, this is a rather good thing to know because it means that you won't panic if you discover this. People who suffer from chronic anxiety are always in doubt about this relationship between what I feel is *myself* and what I feel is *something else*.

Let's suppose you are anxious about your relationship with other people. You walk into a room and there's some stranger opposite to you, and you know nothing about this stranger, so maybe you feel a little reluctant to open conversation. You don't know whether this person is going to be sane, or some kind of a crackpot, or some kind of an awful, stuffy square, or who knows what. So you start fencing around a little, but you get the feeling of "Now, I better watch myself because I do, after all, want to make a good impression; I don't want to make an enemy." So you watch yourself, and this funny thing then begins, called self-consciousness. And also, there is involved in this encounter, the secret games that people are playing all the time to defend themselves by putting other people down. This is really a very wicked game.

Every living being—if the truth be told—is a manifestation of everything that there is, of what we call "God" in old-fashioned language. Every human being is. And as I look around, I can see every one of you as the divine being coming at me in a different way. Crazy! But what we do is to try and prevent people from realizing that this is so by pointing their limitations out to them in the most subtle ways, and seeing if we can faze them—put a person off a little bit, make them uncertain, make them unsteady. It's like the sorts of games you can play where if a person wavers, they lose—where it's absolutely essential to have total nerve in order to win. Supposing I have nerve as a speaker, but there might be someone in this audience that would do something very funny in the background to distract my attention so that I would get worried. And he would make me wonder if my fly buttons are undone, or something like that, and would put me off. He would be playing that little game to try and get in on my nerve.

People play that game with each other all the time, and the reason they do it is not the reason they think—it is that if everybody were perfectly clear that they were a manifestation of the divine being, nothing very much would happen. But so as to keep everybody a little bit unclear about it, the whole thing bugs itself, and creates these little doubts. So what we are beginning with is these little doubts, these sensations of blockage, of not being very sure of yourself, but knowing very much indeed that you are yourself, and you're alone, and it's all up to you—a terrible feeling of responsibility.

What I am trying to point out to you is that if you intensify that feeling, and bring it to its highest pitch, you will immediately realize that you are aware of it only by virtue of the entire sensation of something else—something defined as *not-you*. So the feeling of *not-you* and the feeling of *you* are relative—they go together—and you can't have the one without the other. And if you can't have the one without the other, that means there is a secret conspiracy between the two, and they are really the same, but pretending to be different.

Because the whole idea is if there wasn't a difference, you wouldn't know anything was happening. I mean, if it was all the same, it's like that song of Bob Dylan's which says something like, "Well, I'm just like a guy like you, I'm just like anybody else; no use me talking to you, because you're just like me." So the whole point is, then, if all of us were the same, and all shared the same ideas exactly, and so on, there would be nothing to talk about—because everybody would be a bore. There would be just yourself, echoing back at you, and you would feel like a madman in a hall of mirrors—where everywhere you went was just yourself in all directions—just you. Well, that's no fun.

But you may think that I'm speaking in favor of some kind of schizoid, pluralistic universe. But no, the whole point is this: that difference, and every kind of variety of differentiation, is the way through which unity is discovered. I mean, this business about *vive la petite différence* is very important. And the fact that men and women, for example—as a primordial kind of difference—never can really understand each other, is tremendously exciting. Because that's a way by which something happens. If it makes a difference, then it's there. If it doesn't make a difference, it doesn't matter. And what doesn't matter does not exist, because it has no matter.

However, wherever you notice a difference, the difference has two sides: what it is, and what it's not. And these two sides, since you cannot have the one side without the other side, they are really one—because they *go together*, inseparably. So, when you get this extreme sense of your own existence as a rather painful fact in the middle of everything else, the "everything else" feeling and the "you" feeling are two poles of one and the same process. So that *the real you* is what lies, as it were, between these poles and includes both of them.

Now, this is the fundamental principle of the whole way in which ancient Chinese thought developed—the philosophy of the *yang* and the *yin*. This is one of the oldest ideas of this planet. And the philosophy, which I shall have occasion to speak of a little bit more later, of the *Book of Changes* (the *I Ching*), is based entirely on the view that the universe is the interplay of difference. And the primordial difference is between up and down, back and front, black and white, is and isn't, male and female, positive and negative. So the word *yang* in Chinese refers to the south side of a mountain, which is the sunny side. The word *yin* refers to the north side of the mountain, which is the shady side. Did you ever see a south-sided mountain, with no north side? Or *yang* may also refer to the north bank of a river, which gets the sun, and *yin* to the south bank of the river, which gets the shade.

And so you will remember this great *yin-yang* symbol. One half, of course, is colored dark—as it were, two fishes interlocked, chasing each other. You see more complicated symbols in which they form a helix, and the spiral nebulae are shaped this way. Fundamentally, this is the position of man and woman making love, where I am trying to get inside you and you are trying to get inside me; we are trying to get into the middle of each other, but somehow or other, there is a difference, and we can never quite get there. Just like, if I want to see the back of my head, I can go round and round and I can chase it, but I never quite catch up with it. But that's what makes everything work. It is said in the Vedanta sutras, that the Lord—the supreme knower of all things, who is the knower in all of us—does not know itself in the same way that fire does not burn itself, and a knife does not cut itself. So even to God, nothing would be more mysterious than God.

You know how you surprise yourself sometimes? For example, when you feel your own pulse and you suddenly notice there's life going on in you, which you're not willing. Or, say, you have the belly rumbles; you didn't intend to have the belly rumbles, but suddenly it happened. Or you had hiccups. Now, are you having hiccups or not? Is this something you are *doing*? Or is it merely something that's *happening* to you? (As if it was raining, and the rain was happening to you.) This is a very debatable question. Consider breathing: Are *you* breathing? Or is it breathing you? Well, you can feel it either way. You can decide to breathe, and feel that you're breathing—just in the same way that you walk when you want to. On the other hand, when you forget about breathing altogether it still goes on, and so it seems to be something that happens to you. Which is it? Do you grow your hair, or does your hair just grow by itself? And what enables you to make a decision? When you decide, do you first decide to decide, or do you just decide? Now, how do you do that? Nobody knows, you see.

When Chuang-tzu tells the story that one philosopher asked another, "How can one get the Tao, so as to have it for one's own?" the other philosopher answers:

> Your life is not your own. It is the delegated adaptability of Tao. Your offspring are not your own. They are the outputs of Tao. You move, you know not how. You are at rest, you know not why. These are the operations of Tao. So how could you have it for your own?

It's a funny thing that we can experience ourselves through and through as something that just happens. Look at it this way: If you feel your body, your skin, and the solidity of yourself, and regard what marvelous eyes you have—which are the power that generates light and color out of all these electrical quanta in the external world—and these ears, these beautiful shells that you wear on the side of your head, with their little spiral bones (the cochlear inside), all that is marvelous, but you don't feel responsible for this. You don't know how it's made—if it is *made*—but it's you! That's what you are—that extraordinary pattern, beautiful, gorgeous, wonderful arabesque of tubes, and bones, and cartilage, and myriads of interconnecting electronics, and nervous systems, and everything so wonderful.

But the point is, most people don't own this; they don't say, "This is me." They say, "Well, it's some kind of very clever machine which the Lord God made out of his infinite wisdom, and put me inside it." And this is a very limited view. Because the extraordinary thing is, that this is you—all these extraordinary, marvelous goings on. But you can feel it, all of it, as if it was just happening to you. But if you want to feel it that way, then you have got to go the whole way and you've got to feel that *your decisions just happen to you*, and that the thing that you call your "self"—to which things happen—is also something that happens. You don't know how you manage to be an ego, how you happen to be conscious—that just happens too. So happenings happen to a happening. And so you can feel yourself completely irresponsible, like that. When you get that way, that is a very interesting road to run.

But you can try the other way; you can extend it and say, "If I really am my eyes, and although I don't understand them (that is to say, I can't describe it in lines and words) this is me." It's an extraordinary thing, yet I don't understand how it happens. But then, you see, that's the whole point I made a little while ago—that the very Lord God himself doesn't understand how it happens. Because if he did, what would be the point? There would be no mystery; there would be no possibility of surprises.

That's why there has to be *yang* and *yin*. *Yang* is bright, and it understands everything. *Yin* is dark, and damned if she will be understood. But they are two phases of the same being, and so your *yang* side is your conscious attention: all the bright things you know, and all the information you have, and all the know-how. And your *yin* side is the other side of the *yang*, which enables the *yang* to function. Because you really don't know why the *yang* side of you functions—that is, the conscious, bright, intelligent side of you—it all depends on something you don't understand at all. And if it didn't, it wouldn't be there—just like you wouldn't be here unless there was something else. So they move together.

And therefore, if you will accept the idea that you *are* your own eyes, and your own heart, and your own ears with that wonderful little spiral cochlear inside, and all these amazing gadgets here—you are all that. You don't know anything about it, but you are it. Now, therefore, by a little extension of the imagination, you can very well see that if all those bones and subtleties inside you feel *other* than your conscious ego—but nevertheless are one with it—the same argument will go for all the other things going on around you: the sun shining, the stars twinkling, the wind blowing, and the great ocean restlessly pounding against the cliffs. That's you too. You don't control it, of course, because there has to be something about you that you don't control, or you wouldn't be you.

Now you see, all that is lesson elementary in relativity. And I have talked about relativity in this way that is kind of unscholarly and so on, but I wanted to get the idea across, because to understand the principle of relativity is the absolute foundation of the philosophy of the Tao. Lao-tzu takes it up in his second chapter, when he says:

When all the world understands beauty to be beautiful,
  there is already ugliness;
When all the world understands goodness to be good,
  there is already evil.
Thus, "to be" and "not to be" arise mutually;
High and low are positive mutually;
Long and short are compared mutually.

And he goes through a whole list of opposites and shows how they create each other. It's like that wonderful little parable, that the Chinese character for "man" looks more or less like an upturned "v." Lafcadio Hearn, in one of his books, tells a story of a Japanese girl telling her little sister the meaning of the character for "man," by taking two sticks of firewood and balancing them together on the ground so that they form the upturned "v." And she says to her little sister, "This is the character for 'man,' because neither stick will stand up unless it has the other to help it." But the profound meaning underneath this is there is no self without other.

To get back to the original point, every creature in the world feels it's a man. (I don't mean a male, but a human.) And that is because, it is in this situation where the thing it feels as *itself*—as its separate identity—is supported by the equal and opposite sensation of "other." Center, periphery; here, there; now, then; is, isn't; and so on. These two are the *yang* and the *yin*—the two poles that hold each other up. So the Zen poem says, "When misfortune comes, treat it as a blessing; when fortune comes, treat it as a disaster."

CHAPTER FIVE

BEING IN THE WAY II

What I was doing yesterday was establishing as the foundation of the philosophy of the Tao, the principle of relativity, and I explained that this was the one absolutely important thing you had to understand in order to get the whole point of what this is about. And all this relativity theory is an explication of the Tao, or the Way, or course of nature. This idea of Tao—the flow of life—is really very, very basic to Chinese thinking, and is becoming very basic to our thinking too, because we are more and more aware of the fact that the universe is an energy system. That is to say, it is not an amalgamation of block entities called "things"; it is not based, as the Newtonian universe was based, on the analogy of billiards.

The original idea of an atom is something which is *atomas*, which means "undividable," or "uncuttable." And so in this way you had to feel that if there was material in the world, if there was matter, then you finally are eventually going to get down to an absolutely uncuttable crumb. But you know how children divide up the last piece of cake, and you can chop a cake and then you can divide it again and divide it again and divide it again—although with very fine instruments you can still cut that—we can go down and down until there will be something so fundamentally hard and so tiny that there will be no way of cutting it at all, and that is the original *atom*. And in Newton and Descartes' theory of the universe, these little billiard balls were banging each other around, and everything could be explained by cosmic billiards.

Until along comes twentieth century physics, which shows that these atoms are not uncuttable at all, but that they are made in an extraordinary way. In fact, perhaps "made" is quite the wrong word to use for them. When Sir Arthur Eddington, many years ago, discussed the nature of electrons in his book, *The Nature of the Physical World*, he said the time has passed when we even ask the question what an electron is. Something unknown is doing we don't know what—that is what our theory amounts to. So in other words, the transformation which took place in Western thought was this: that the operation of nature is not produced by the operation of force and energy upon stuff, or matter.

That was thinking about the universe by analogy with ceramics, and you don't need to think about it that way. Although the ancient Hebrews did, and gave us the idea of God creating Adam by making a clay figurine and then blowing the breath of life into his nostrils. Aristotle compounded this with his *form* and *matter*, and so ever afterwards it has become common sense for almost every European-speaking people to think that the world is fundamentally "shaped stuff." And *stuff* by itself is obviously stupid, like clay; and therefore it needs to be in-formed by spirit or energy.

But today we don't think about this in this way at all. We think of the universe as a system of energy, and the energy flows in such a way as in a rock to act hard, and in water to act liquid, and in air to act pretty soft and gassy, and so all the way around. Everything is pattern of energy. But I don't want you to think of the words "pattern of energy" as if the pattern were one thing and the energy another—as if a pattern were a thing *made* of something called "energy." Energy and pattern are the same thing because you will never find energy not in a pattern or a pattern that is not energy. And if these things are inextricably associated, you can be sure there is some sort of conspiracy underneath the whole thing, and that they are really one.

So then, the course of the world is a constant flow. I used the analogy last night of each person being like a whirlpool in a stream. Now, as you watch it, the form of a whirlpool remains fairly constant, but the water never stays in it. So in exactly the same way, all things, all people, all plants, and whatsoever there is, is a form of constant change; it's changing perpetually, but it's changing in a certain dance. And the form of the dance remains constant until you get bored with it, or it falls apart.

Now, we are sort of hypnotized by our social institutions and conventions into thinking that any given form of energy exists by itself, and that *I*, for example, am a tremendously important person who has to be looked after and watched and protected from dying, going broke, and all that sort of thing. So I have to protect this thing as if somehow or other, if I fail in protecting this particular display of energy, all is lost. Well it isn't. But we are taught to think that way. And you can be untaught. In other words, your mind can be wiped clean, and you can experience yourself as a whirlpool of energy in a stream which is the Tao, which is the total course of nature—the energy field of the whole cosmos.

And so the objective, if you might call it that, of the Taoist way of life, the Taoist discipline, is to enable people to feel that way—to become transparent to yourself. In other words, to feel that you are, just like anything else around you, something through which life is flowing, and you're sort of transparent. You don't constitute a block in it—like you swallowed something and it got stuck in your throat, or that constitutes a block in the alimentary tract. Or if you take a worm and bruise it, the worm wiggles on either side of the bruise, but it can't make a wave wiggle through the whole length of its body.

There was a very strange man called Wilhelm Reich, who said that most people have a thing like the worm's bruise across their diaphragm, so that they find difficulty in wiggling all the way through. So in exactly this way, Taoism teaches you to wiggle all the way through—not only from foot to head, but from one end of space to the other. You are a wiggle in the middle of that—but let it happen, you see. And so this then—to learn how to be with the wiggle—is to be in the Tao.

But you do have here, you see, the idea of an intelligence that is rhythmic: that goes on and off, that pulses. Intelligent, yes, but this is in a curious way quite different from our idea of God. And it is very important to understand at the beginning, the difference between the Tao and God. The idea of God in the West has a history which is originally political—that is to say, the title with which the Lord is addressed, very often is "King of kings, Lord of lords."

Now, the King of kings (or the *Yan Khan*) is a Persian term, which was applied to the Persian emperors. The word *Cyrus* is not a personal name, it means "the Lord"—it's the same as the Greek *Kyrios*. So the idea of the great Persian emperors—or before them the Chaldean emperors and the Egyptian pharaohs, these tremendous potentate—was the original model of the Hebrew idea of *Yahweh*. He is the ruler in heaven, and so all creatures below him obey his orders. For one of the great things that all these Near Eastern emperors did was to issue laws. And so the laws of the Medes and Persians, you know, the thing about them—why they are always referred to as sort of fundamental laws—was they could never be repealed. And so you have the Code of Hammurabi, and you have the Law of Moses, which is based on the Code of Hammurabi. So here is the model of the whole Hebrew-Christian notion of God, the one who lays down the laws of nature, who gives you the Word. The Word is the law, the commandment. "By the Word of the Lord were the heavens made; and all the hosts of them, by the breath of His mouth."

Now, the Chinese simply do not have that conception of the universe. In their thinking, they do have a word for "law" as we use it—that is to say, positive law, rules—and this word is *tse*. The original form of this word resembles a sacrificial cauldron with a knife beside it, because in very ancient times there was a certain emperor who did write down laws for the people, and what he did was he had them engraved on the big iron cauldrons to which the people brought sacrifices, so that when they brought the sacrifice they would read the laws. But his sages said this was a very bad idea, because once you write the law down people will develop a litigious spirit. They will say, "But it doesn't say *this*. It isn't specific about *that*," and so come lawyers and all the complications that follow.

A good judge is a reasonable person, and has this absolutely necessary quality, which is called approximately, *jen*, in Chinese—and that means "human-heartedness." That means being a reasonable human being—after all, come off it, you can be reasonable! And so it is a spirit of compromise, of balancing things out, and of generally muddling through. So, the model of the political ruler who gives orders is not suitable for the idea of Tao. In one chapter of the *Tao Te Ching*, Lao-tzu says this of the Tao:

The great Tao flows everywhere,
both to the left and to the right,
It loves and nourishes all things,
but does not lord it over them.
And when merits are accomplished,
it lays no claim to them.

Now you see, the Western God—in the popular literature, at any rate—is always laying claim to things. People bow down before the Lord and say, "Any good that I have done is of you, and all the evil I have done is of me," and "You, God, ought to be thanked for everything; you have given us this, you have given us that, you have given us the other," and so on. And so you feel that the Lord is sitting up there and receiving all these compliments—just like the Oriental potentate—and may receive them very graciously; but nevertheless, these compliments are definitely in order.

Now for the Taoist philosophy, you have to get used to the idea of thinking of nature as a system which has no boss. That is absolutely fundamental, and that's why the word for nature is *tzu-jan*, or "what is so of itself." It's almost means automatic, except that the word *automatic* in English has a mechanical feel. But in the same way your heart beats without your having to govern it—it does it of itself—so the Taoist view of the universe is that everything happens by itself. And yet, just because everything happens of itself, and you leave it alone and don't try to push it around, it is orderly.

Now, this is a very democratic theory. I cannot understand for the life of me how people can be members of a republic like the United States, and think that this is the best form of government, and yet hold to a monarchical theory of the universe. If the universe is a monarchy, then that is obviously the best form of government, and you ought to have a monarchy here. But you don't, because you had bad experience in past times under the British and other kinds of rulers, and to hell with all that. You are going to be self-governing. Well, to be self-governing you have to have a measure of anarchy—in other words, you have to trust other people. And this is a country because it consists of people who originally lived under monarchies and found it very difficult to trust other people.

This is the most paranoid country on earth, and it's always saying *there ought to be a law against it*, and stopping other people from doing this, that, and the other—just terrified that they may run amok. But if you want to live in a democracy, you have to take the risk of your neighbor running amok, because democracy is simply based on trusting your neighbor—even though he may be a crook. Otherwise, you have to have a police state and you are back to a monarchy of some kind. Whether the individual in charge is one person or a committee, it makes no difference; that's what you get back to if you won't trust your fellow man.

So then, in the Taoist theory of the universe everything is "let go." It's as if God had said, "Now, I am producing everything, but I am going to disappear—be invisible and just not there—and let everything happen according to its nature." And yet, the thing is, the more you let go, the more things begin to work. This is one of those interesting paradoxes of which Taoism is full. When you consider, for example, the human organism as a totality—and remember we were discussing in the last session whether the brain was made for the stomach, or the stomach was made for the brain—or in other words, who is in charge around here? Well, the truth of the matter is, nobody is in charge. And in the end, the brain and the stomach are not really different; they have the same relationship to each other as bees and flowers do.

Otherwise there wouldn't be any flowers unless there were bees; there wouldn't be any bees unless there were flowers. Nothing could look more different than a bee and a flower, and yet, they are a unified organism. Nothing could look more different than head and feet, and yet, it's a single organism. It happens to be tied together in a certain way, so you can see that it's one. But now, bees and flowers are tied by things that are not quite so visible to us; although they are very visible to a bee. They sense all sorts of subtle currents in the air, along which drift the smells of flowers, and these connect flowers with bees just as effectively as our spinal column connects our head with our hips. So the bee and the flower is a unified organism; one part of it does not exist without the other part.

And so, one can't say which came the first, bee or flower? It's like which came the first, egg or hen? In the Chinese way of saying it, they "arise mutually." The Chinese character for this consists of two phrases: one means "mutual" or "reciprocal," and the other is originally an image of a growing plant of some kind, and means "to arise," "to grow," "to produce," or "to be born." So the world is seen as a system in which all the pairs of opposites and all such symbiotic group relationships arise mutually—as you get with bees and flowers, in-groups and out-groups, heads and tails of cats, eggs and birds, etc. That simply means that they are aspects of one and the same pattern, and it comes into being together.

Now, it may sound odd to say that *you as an individual arise mutually with the rest of the universe*—but you do! And it's very important to realize this, because it is the key to understanding your own individuality. Let me, first of all, make it plain from a purely physiological point of view: the world that you see outside you is a state of your own nervous system. In other words, it is because you have senses and a nervous organization of a certain structure that the sky is blue, that the sun is light, and that vibrations in the air are sound. You turn them into color, light, sound, etc. Because supposing I hit a drum which has no skin, there is no noise. So if air vibrates and pulses but doesn't encounter an eardrum, there is no sound. That is the answer to the old problem of a tree falling in a forest (whether it makes a noise if nobody is around to hear). The answer is it doesn't, but it makes vibrations in the air, and again, we only know that if there is something to measure them.

A Zen poem says, "The tree shows the bodily power of the wind." And so if the wind blows across nothing, nobody knows it's blowing. But if there's some sand lying around, and the sand gets up and drifts, then you see the wind. In the same way, the sun can shine and shine and shine, but if there are no planets to reflect the light, space will be full of darkness. It takes two. It takes *you*, as an individual sensitive organism with the particular structure of nerves that you have, to evoke what we call *nature* and *the external world*.

You might wonder: What is it outside that we evoke in this way? Well, the physicists will say, "Oh, it is a system of electricity, of quanta, and so on." But that is only what they see through using their instruments. In other words, what's outside in relation to certain instruments that a physicist may use is described in terms of electrical vibrations or quanta. If you analyze any scientific language—electricity, for example, it comes down to a big, completely superstitious Greek expression, some mysterious force. That's all it means, as when doctors will say a person has neuritis, which simply means that their nerves hurt. So watch out for these scientists—even they may not know what it is. They can measure it, yes; they can number it, and by measuring and numbering its behavior patterns they can predict what it will do next, to an extent.

The point is, that you, as a pattern of energy—which we call *the physical body*—you evoke the external world. But at the same moment, you are something *in* the external world. Each one of you is in my external world and I am in your external world. We are simultaneously in the external world, and yet we are evoking the external world—turning it into color, and shape, and hardness, and softness, and hot, and cold, and all these things that we recognize. So the existence of the external world, as anything that can be thought about or imagined, is created by the structure of your organism; and in turn, the structure of your organism is a function of the external world. There is a reciprocal relationship—or what we might call a *transaction*—between you as an organism and the universe.

So in this sense we could say, that if the universe were not here, you would not be here; if you were not here, the universe would not be here—and that direction is rather more difficult to understand. Because you may say, "Presumably I was born at a certain time and I will die at a certain time; before I was born the universe was there, and after I am dead the universe will still be there for others; how then can you say that *the whole universe* depends on me?" Well, that is very simple, indeed. It depends on you not as something that lasts *all* the time, but it depends on you having been there *some* of the time. In other words, eternity is related to the temporal. We contrast the eternal and the temporal as a set of opposites, and we could not have eternity without temporality, and we cannot have temporality without eternity.

The fact that Socrates existed tells us a great deal about the world. If the world is capable of Socrates-ing, it makes it much more interesting. You see, the world once Buddha-ed, it Jesus-ed, and it shows us the potentialities within the world that these beings did exist. And so, insofar as any manifestation of nature is symptomatic of nature, it shows us that the whole is expressed here—and I won't say as a *part*, because I don't regard individuals as parts of nature—like you cut up a pie and have parts of it. Individuals are all expressions of nature. So going back, the whole universe depends on the temporal existence of every single one of its expressions.

And this in Buddhist philosophy is called (in Japanese) *ji-ji-mu-ge*—that is to say, the mutual interpenetration of all things and events. Imagine a spider's web and the dew of dawn upon it, and you look at this web and you see, in every little drop of dew, the reflection of all the other drops of dew. And if you look closer still, in every other drop of dew reflected in the first drop of dew, you will see, again, the reflections of all the other drops of dew, and so ad infinitum. And this is the great Mahayana Buddhist diagram or model of the universe: each one contains everything.

You may be under the influence of a certain kind of nineteenth century nonsense, which said, *man is, after all, only a tiny little microbe on an extremely unimportant planet, revolving around a minor star on the fringes of one of the smaller galaxies.* What a put-down! But how exciting that this being, in just that unimportant sort of position, discovers that they can evoke the whole thing with their amazing body. And furthermore, ever since Einstein started scratching his head, it is quite legitimate to regard any place in the universe as the center of it.

If you take the surface of a sphere, and suppose that space is curved, where is the center of the surface of the sphere? Well, it's anywhere you choose. All you have to do is put your finger on it and then move that position so that it lines up with your vision. Take, for example, a mirror ball and look at it. You will always find that however you rotate it, the center of the mirror sphere is facing you, and wherever you look at it you will be in the middle. So, any point in the universe can be regarded as truly the center.

So there is no reason why we shouldn't go back in an entirely new way to a kind of Ptolemaic theory of the universe—but a sophisticated Ptolemaic theory based on twentieth century science, where we are still in the center, because we know now that space is curved. Do you know what the pathetic fallacy is? The pathetic fallacy is the projection of human feelings, intelligence, and emotions upon non-human objects. *The sea is sighing. The wind in the pine trees sounds sad. The sun is happy today.* All that sort of thing is called the pathetic fallacy, but it's not so inaccurate after all. What they wanted to prove in the nineteenth century was that intelligence resides *only* inside human skins, and that everything else outside is blind force, brute energy, dumb matter, and generally stupid. They could not see, at that point, that a human being is symptomatic of their environment, and expresses their environment. So if you are intelligent, you are in an intelligent environment—there's no other way to it.

Well, then, today we see differently. We realize that everything that we see is human. That is to say, all that is outside us whatsoever is known to us by being translated into the shape of our brains, and therefore is humanized. You may think it anthropomorphic to conceive God as an old gentleman with a white beard sitting on a golden throne, but it is just as anthropomorphic to consider the nature of the universe in the formula $E = mc^2$. Because that too, is a human, rational conception; it's completely human, anthropomorphic (i.e., *of the form of man).*

So everywhere you see a human universe in relation to which you exist, and it exists in relation to you. And it's as big as big can be, and you are as small as small can be. And it's as long as long can be, and goes on forever and ever, while you go on for a limited time only. But just as difference exemplifies unity, so brevity emphasizes and brings out length. And time, therefore, brings out eternity—just in the same way a figure brings out a background, and a background is necessary for bringing out a figure.

So then, the Tao process is not one of government. The relationship between *you* as the little fellow and *the universe* as the enormous thing is not one of hierarchy—it's not that political model. It is mutuality, where there is an accord to move together—like dancers who are wonderfully partnered so that you don't know which one is leading and which one is following; they just read each other's minds. And that is how you act in concord with your environment: you arise together. Though not necessarily in time, because it may start long before you arrived—just as the tree is growing before it produces any fruit. But fruit is implied in the tree, so people are implied in the cosmos. And so, as it were, you are there from the beginning, by implication, just as the apple is implicit in the apple tree.

Now when you find a relationship like that, where the two aspects of it—the great and the small, the vast and long and the little and short—and you don't find one without the other, then you know this is not a separation, but a union. Where what we call the *long* is one end of the same energy pattern of which *short* is the other end. Imagine a triangle: it has a wide base and a tiny point. Well, that's the nature of a triangle. And imagine the ocean: the waves come, and the waves go, but the ocean keeps on waving. Well, we are similarly like that. No ocean without waves, you know—it's a dynamic system, it's moving. And so, we are the universe waving—each one of us is it waving in a particular way.

So what you do—if you want to find that out—is you have to deepen your consciousness. You have to go down to its roots and discover the point where it ceases to be purely you, where it ceases to be simply the system of memories and habits that you call your "ego." And underneath that system, which is, as it were, the crest of the wave, deep down underneath that is the huge force of the ocean, which is present in you at all times, operating at the basis of your consciousness—which is at the same time the basis of your physical energy, muscular power, and indeed, existence at all.

But at that level you are supra-personal. That is to say, when you realize that you stand here as a body because you had a father and mother, and they passed on to you those genes, those DNA and RNA tricks that produce you here as a physical entity; and of course, your father and mother had parents, and it goes way, way, way back. It's as if there was—according to certain cosmological theories today—a primordial explosion which blew up and created the universe. And you know how it is when you take a bottle of ink and you throw it at a whitewashed wall and it goes *splash* all over the place: there is a big blob in the center, and then as it goes out, it gets all sorts of little curlicues and wiggles. So you see, the cosmic explosion is still happening. It takes a long time from that big central *bang* for the whole thing to go *whoosh*; it takes billions of years for it to expand, and it is still happening. We are the little curlicues out on the edge of that. But also, we are connected, we are part of the central explosion that originally happened. That in a certain sense is *in you*—you are still manifesting it.

So when you consider yourself as a physical being, consider your hand: it is very ancient. Just like when you pick up a stone, and say, "How old is this stone?" Scientists will say, "Well, it comes from the Pleistocene Age and it's probably four million years old." But then you think, "Well, wait a minute, wait a minute, wait a minute! What do you mean four million years old? Where did it come from? What was it before it was a stone?" Well, it was something or other, and that goes back, back, back, you see?

So everything you touch, including yourself, is incredibly ancient; it goes back to the very beginning of time. So if your mind awakens, you suddenly see all your friends sitting around you, looking incredibly ancient. I don't mean in the sense of old and haggard, but like angels—like eternal beings—who were always there from the beginning.

CHAPTER SIX

BEING IN THE WAY III

Once upon a time there was a Chinese farmer who lost a horse; it ran away. And all the neighbors came round that evening and said, "That's too bad."

And he said, "Maybe."

The next day the horse came back and brought seven wild horses with it, and all the neighbors came around and said, "Why, that's great, isn't it?"

And he said, "Maybe."

The next day, while attempting to tame one of these horses, his son was thrown and broke his leg. And all the neighbors came round in the evening and said, "Well, that's too bad, isn't it?"

And the farmer said, "Maybe."

And the next day, the conscription officers came around looking for people for the army, and they rejected his son because he had a broken leg. And all the neighbors came round that evening and said, "Isn't that wonderful?"

And he said, "Maybe."

This in a certain sense, reflects a fundamentally Taoistic attitude, which is that the whole process of nature is an integrated process of immense complexity, and it is really impossible to tell whether anything that happens in it is good or bad. Because you never know what will be the consequences of a misfortune, or you never know what will be the consequences of good fortune. I know a woman who was quite happy until she inherited two million dollars, and then she became absolutely miserable because she was afflicted with paranoia that everybody was going to take it away from her, especially the government.

And on the other hand, you have all known cases where some sort of ridiculous inconvenience or accident preserved you from a worse one. Or else, it was an occasion on which you met someone you fell in love with or formed a fast friendship. You never know what the chain, the pattern, the connection between events may be. And it is for this reason that the Taoist has been critical of two things: of words, and of interference.

He criticizes words, because among the Confucians—who were always literary people—they had a thing going called the *rectification of names*. Now I have to introduce this by way of a little observation about Confucians in general, because they have their positive and their negative side, but their negative side is their rather exclusive interest in matters literary. In the history of Chinese civilization no kind of real scientific advances came through Confucian studies because they were scholastics. That is to say, a scholastic is one who knows what is in the book, believes what the ancient texts or scriptures say, studies them, and becomes proficient, like a rabbi or a Christian theologian.

But mystics are not interested very much in theology. All mystics are interested in direct experience; and therefore, although you may laugh at them and say they are not scientific, they are empirical in their approach. And the Taoists, being mystics, were the only great group of ancient Chinese people that seriously studied nature. They were interested in it from the beginning, and their books are full of analogies between the principles of the Taoist way of life and the behavior of natural forces, of water, wind, plants, and rocks. In many passages Lao-tzu likens the Tao to water—in the fact that it does not resist and yet nothing is stronger, and in the fact that it always takes the line of least resistance—and that it always seeks the lowest level, which men abhor. Many things are said about water, and many things are said about plants. And many things are said about the processes of growth, about wind—how wind plays music with all the orifices and openings in nature, and blows through them and brings out their particular hum.

Strangely enough, it was from the Taoists that Chinese people developed as much science as they did, but they never developed anything like Western technology. And there are many reasons—some of them purely geographical—but one of the reasons why the Chinese did not go on to develop an advanced technology had to do with names, and it had to do with a certain attitude to nature. Now, so far as names are concerned, the Taoists always laughed at the idea of the rectification of names because they said, "Now look, when you compile a dictionary, you define your words with other words. With what other words are you going to define the words with which you define the words—so as to be sure you have got them straight?"

I remember when I was a small boy, I wanted to write a book which would forever preserve the fundamentals of human knowledge. So the first thing I wrote down in it was the alphabet. And then I scratched my head regarding how I would write down how to pronounce each of these letters. I tried to spell out in letters how to pronounce letters, not realizing of course that this was a completely vicious circle. In order to understand words you have to have something else—and that is a very mysterious matter. In the kind of understanding that we have of things which we then go on to describe in words, one realizes how much one learns as a child—especially from other people—which is never explicitly stated. How do you know, for example, whether somebody who says something to you is serious or kidding? A great deal of confusion is caused by that, even among adults. And how the processes have been examined and analyzed and studied, which are required for understanding the simplest sentence, and yet we don't know how the brain of a child accomplishes this extraordinary task—which when an analyst looks at it, is extremely complicated.

But of course, you must realize that analysis is a way of making things complicated that were not complicated in the first place. And it was like my task that I set myself as a child: the amazingly complicated task of how to write down how the letters were pronounced. Now, a great deal of academic energy goes into this task of proving things that everybody knows. But they want to say precisely, what thing is it that you know? How can we delimit it? How can we pin it down, *exactly*? And this, of course, is very much involved also with law, and that's why you say things like "I devise," "I bequeath," "I give," etc.—so that there can be absolutely no doubt about what you mean.

But as a matter of fact, the trouble is, the more definite you become with words in describing something, the more doubt you create. And so the Taoist took a profoundly humorous attitude to the Confucian's interest in spelling things out—because they said you can never do it. It is an entirely circular process, it's simply a self-defining affair. So that when I pick up a Chinese dictionary, or better still for my purposes, supposing I pick up a Finnish dictionary—which has nothing in it but Finnish language—it doesn't tell me a thing, because I haven't got the key. And the key to this language is not altogether communicable in language. So for this reason, then, the Taoist was thoroughly skeptical of the power of words to describe the processes of the physical world.

Now, the Chinese language as such, is a rather peculiar language—unlike most other languages in that it neither declines its nouns nor conjugates its verbs. There are certain ways, sometimes, of showing whether a verb indicates the future or whether it indicates the past, but in general, literally translated Chinese reads like a telegram. And so the opening of the chapter of the Lao-tzu book on *te*—that is to say, on "power" or "virtue"—says in literal English, "Superior te, not te; thus, this has te. Inferior te, not let go of virtue; thus, this not virtue." This says it so succinctly, but we have to go bubbling around and say, "The superior form of virtue is not conscious of itself as virtue, and thus truly is virtue; but the inferior form of virtue so insists on being virtuous that it's not virtue." But that's a very complicated way of saying things, whereas the Chinese says it so pithily.

But on the other hand, the Chinese language, which is not specific in this way that we can be by declining nouns and conjugating verbs exactly—what, how, and to whom—we have a better language. (And so do the Japanese, because they have an arrangement for using Chinese in such a way as to decline the nouns and conjugate the verbs.) We have a better language for describing technological processes. You know how it is when you get a set of instructions to put something together: First, do *this*, then do *that*, then do *the other thing*. But when you get a Chinese product from Hong Kong with instructions to put it together, you just have to know how it's done before you read it. But the compensatory delight of this language is that you can say several things at once, and mean them all.

However, the point that we go on to now is the second one, the question of interference. With this realization—that language is a net which will never succeed in capturing the world—goes a reluctance to interfere with the processes of nature. Because what you think may be a good thing to do may be good only in the short run; it may turn out to be disastrous in the long run. To give a very simple example, which is very close to the hearts of all Chinese and Asian people: the problem of population. What on earth are we going to do about that? Because in times past the huge populations of India and China were thinned by perennial outbreaks of cholera, other diseases, and famines, which wiped out millions of people, and so the population was balanced.

Now, however, with the methods of modern medicine we begin to stamp out these plagues, but then a new plague turns up in the form of human beings—too many of them. Well, you can't just go around in cold blood getting rid of people who you regard as not making up to certain standards. It was somehow better if the cholera did it, because that was impersonal, and it bore you no spite. But when human beings have to decide to get rid of each other, then there is real trouble.

So a Taoist would be, on the whole, inclined not to interfere with the course of events because he feels that they are of a complexity so great, that he, with his verbal interpretations, doesn't really know in terms of words whether a given event is good or bad. Because all that we call *scientific knowledge* is a verbal interpretation of what is going on, along with a certain selection of things that we call "good" and a selection of certain things that we call "bad." He may feel badly about it, but he may also feel that this is the proper and appropriate way to feel in such circumstances, and that it will go over—it will pass. For as Lao-tzu said, "The fierce gale does not last the whole morning, nor does pelting rain go on all day." (Maybe he hadn't lived in Big Sur, but still, it's true in general.) Then he goes on to say, "If heaven and earth cannot keep up these things for long, how much less can mankind."

This, then, is a basic attitude in Taoist philosophy, which goes by the name of *wu-wei*. *Wu* means "negative" and *wei* means "doing," "interfering," "busyness," "poking into things." So *wu-wei* means "don't interfere" or "don't strive." However, the best meaning of *wu-wei* is "don't force it."

As when, for example, you are opening a lock and the key doesn't seem to turn, if you force it you will just bend the key. So what you have to do is jiggle, pull back and forth—*jiggle, jiggle, jiggle*—until you find the place where the key turns. And that's *wu-wei.*

Wu-wei doesn't mean total passivity. Because, you see, on the other side of the picture about interfering with nature is that you *must interfere*—there is no way of *not* interfering. Even when you look at something you interfere with it. Your very existence is an interference with the environment, from a certain point of view. So there you are, you're stuck with it—everything you do alters the balance. Even if you sit perfectly still, you're still breathing, and that alters the nature of things going on around you. You're exuding temperature, and that changes something. And then when you start eating, and doing all sorts of things like that, you really do start changing things. So you can't avoid interfering, and yet the maxim seems to be *don't interfere*. But better translated, *wu-wei* means "don't force it."

So then, what do you do? In practice you have to interfere as wisely as possible. That is to say, you have to find out how to interfere along the lines in which things are already developing. This is like sailing a boat: it is much smarter to sail than to row, because it takes less energy. You simply use the wind by putting up a sheet. But then, supposing the wind isn't going where you want to go, then you learn to tack, and you keep the wind in your sails all the time; you use the wind to go against the wind—and therefrom comes the idea of judo.

Judo is the Japanese way of saying "the gentle Tao" ("the gentle Way"). In judo, the basic principle of the whole thing is that you are not an attacker. Underneath judo is a deeper philosophy called *aikido*—that is to say, the Way of *aiki*—where you can never be attacked, because when somebody attacks you, you're not there. Or you are there, but in the form of a vacuum, so that the attacker gets sucked in so fast by his own force that he falls over. In judo, one always uses the strength of the opponent to bring about his downfall, though you may add your own strength at a certain point. In other words, when you're throwing someone in judo there is a point when his own strength has taken him beyond the peak. You know, when a thing is falling over it reaches a certain peak where it's gone—it's on the way down—it is at this moment that you add your strength. But the person has to be beyond the falling point, and then only, do you use your strength.

Judo is a development out of the Taoist philosophy—probably by Japanese people, and judo is relatively modern. It came out of all sorts of understandings going back to Chinese ways of doing things, and gradually amalgamated into the form in which we know it today. But it is a basic demonstration of this principle of *wu-wei.*

Wu-wei isn't an attitude of total passivity; it isn't just doing nothing as it literally says, "not do"— but it's really "not force." So the meaning of *wu-wei* is that in every situation, always, you find out which way the wind is blowing and trim your sails to the wind.

Well, now then, how do you know which way the wind is blowing? Obviously, a scientist would say to you, "Well, we have to make a very careful analysis of the situation and find out just what's going on." And then this becomes extremely interesting, because scientists are doing this very seriously now, and they have devised a very important science that we call *ecology*. And in ecology we study the whole complex of relationships which lie between any organism and its environment. And when we get to the ecology of humankind, it is simply fantastic! When you study, for example, the ecology between humans and the world of microbes, and you try to decide what are good guys and bad guys among the microbes, and how to get rid of the bad guys without getting rid of the good guys—and then you realize you need some of the bad guys, otherwise the good guys fall apart. Some of the killers we use on this level of medicine are very much like what DDT is on the level of agriculture—it's too indiscriminate—and it gets too many of the good guys along with the bad guys.

But you become, after a time, very doubtful as to the precise definition of a "good guy" and a "bad guy" because you see, every group, every species, has to have an enemy—that's part of the whole mutual-eating society arrangement of life. If you don't have an enemy, then you start multiplying too much, nothing prunes you. Then you start getting in your own way, because there are too many of you, and you start eating up your all your own supplies of food stuff. Also, you get soft—you're not on the *qui vive,* or lookout, and you develop flabby muscles because you never get involved in a fight. So gradually, the successful group fails. And inevitably the group that has managed to obliterate all its enemies will fall apart.

So what are we to do about that? Part of the whole conceit of present-day international politics is that the United States, with its vast prosperity and enormous facilities for living the lazy life, *must have* an external enemy to get excited about. And so the Cold War is in a way total nonsense—and everybody who's in the know about anything knows it—that, for example, an atomic war between Russia and the United States would simply end the human race. But the populace has to be kept bamboozled, and we keep fighting wars, like in Vietnam, in order to keep everybody excited and in order to make a *fracas* and to give the soldiers practice. It's a horrible business, but that's the way things run. So the question is, *Can we run the human race without awful bloodshed, and murders, and tortures, and all that kind of thing? Can we somehow introduce a new kind of gamesmanship as a substitute for war?*

It's the same thing in business—exactly. If you wipe out your competitor, then you have no reason to produce anything but a lousy product. And then you may make lots of money because you wiped out your competitors—you've got the whole market. Then you got this money, but what are you going to buy with it? Well, there's nothing to buy except other people's lousy products, who wiped out their competitors, or who cheated the public by packaging the thing to look elegant, but nothing much was inside. That's all you've got to buy. So naturally, if you are a success at General Motors you go and buy a Rolls-Royce from England, or you go and buy a Mercedes from Germany—because they happen to be better cars. Or if you want to make a lot of money in the clothing industry here making wretched prints, and you want some good clothes, what do you do? Well, you have to go to Mexico, and buy the things peasants wear because they are still substantial, well-made, good clothes. So you see, there is something always self-defeating in these attempts to succeed. You could even say that *nothing fails like success.*

So for this reason, then, the Taoist always had an attitude of caution. "Cautiously," Lao-tzu says, "as one who crosses a river in spring." That means either, because of the spring floods or because the ice is still there, and you're not quite sure how strong it is because it's beginning to thaw. So what the Taoist tries to develop is a sensibility to the situation. He tries to feel out—intuitively—what kind of action is required under these circumstances, because he feels that he can never discover it analytically, with his conscious attention alone.

Well now, to talk in modern Western terms about how this is done we must realize, of course, that we are equipped inside our heads with an absolutely fantastic thing called *the brain.* With its millions and millions of neuron cells it is, as it were, the most amazing computer ever devised. Basic to the Taoist attitude to life is that you have that within you, and you may—if you don't know very much about brains—call it *intuition* or something of that kind. But you have within you the most amazing logical analyzer that exists in the known world, and the point is to get it to work for you.

But not with conscious attention alone, which can only think of about three things at a time without using a pencil—that is to say, keep three variables in mind at once. Very few people can do four without using a pencil. You can do four if you're a trained musician where you're playing four different lines of a fugue, and keeping four variables in mind at once. With an organist, you can go from four to six because you've got your two feet and they're playing too. But that requires a high amount of training to be able, with conscious attention, to keep that many variables in mind.

But the world around us has infinitely many variables going on in it, yet you can reason out something with your conscious verbal thinking. For example, if you want to draw up a contract in business, you figure out how to write it, whether it will be a good contract, whether it will work, etc., and you think of all these things, and writing them down you make the contract, and you think that's fine. But one of the variables that you couldn't possibly include in the contract was that your partner would slip on a banana skin and break his neck. I mean, the contract might make provisions in it if your lawyer was thoughtful about what was to be done "under the case of the disability of any of the parties thereto," etc. But eventually there are so many possibilities that can occur that you cannot think of them all.

So then the question arises: *Is it within the power of the human brain to comprehend—with its immense complexity—in a kind of un- or sub-conscious way what the surface consciousness can never grasp?* And the Taoist would say, certainly it can—that you've got to learn to use your brain by allowing it to go to work on your problems without interfering with it, and then it will deliver you a decision. And this is why, when you get into the real study of Taoist and Zen Buddhist practice, you get to the point where you learn to act without making decisions—or rather, to use a more exact word, without *choosing*. Krishnamurti talks a great deal about being "choicelessly aware," and says that freedom is precisely the state of not having to choose.

Now that sounds quite paradoxical, because we're always talking about freedom of choice, but choice is not a form of freedom in this sense of the word. What is choice in this sense of the word? Choice is the act of hesitation that we make before making a decision; it is a mental wobbling. You know, some people when they take up a pen to write, they don't just write, but they jiggle the pen around undecisively and then start writing. Or a person comes into a room and wonders who to talk to, and is sort of in doubt. In that moment he's choosing, whereas a person who comes into a room and decides who to approach doesn't wait to choose. We say he is "decisive," but that's a funny saying because it means he didn't stop to decide.

So in the training in Zen Buddhism, which is simply a Buddhist extension of Taoism (Zen Buddhism arose out of the marriage of Buddhism and Taoism in the fifth century CE and over the following centuries) they have a way of training you so that you always act without choosing. For example, there was one day a leaky roof, and there were a couple of monks attending the Zen master, and he said, "The roof is leaking." One monk disappeared and came back instantly with a sieve and put it under the drips. Another monk, after some time, came back with a bucket. The master praised the one who brought the sieve. Now, the action wasn't exactly appropriate to catching rain, but the point was that he was in the spirit of the Zen discipline by acting without choosing. And you will notice this with certain people who never hesitate. If something needs to be done, they seem somehow simply to grab something and do it, which is a kind of a Zen capacity.

So, what happens is this: the teacher of Zen constantly throws curves at his students, and puts them in dilemma situations where they have to act immediately. One of the things, of course, that you must not do is rush, because rushing is a form of hesitation. When a person rushes to get a train they start to fall over their own feet, so it really holds them up; it's like trying to drive at high speed through the water with a blunt-nosed boat—that's rush. But now, what the Zen master is trying to get is a kind of a smooth, unhesitating, flowing action that is the response to the challenge—and it must be done with what is called *mu*. This is called *wu-nien* in Chinese (or *mu-nen* in Japanese), and the word *nien* is composed of the character meaning "now" and the character meaning "mind-heart" (*hsin*), and so has the meaning of "a thought." But especially for us, it is well translated by the psychological term *blocking*. "You are blocking," you say to someone when they hesitate, when they dither, when they stop to choose. So the attitude of *mu-nen* or *wu-nien* is the unblocked mind—where it does not hesitate, ever. Just as the river doesn't hesitate when it flows, and just as when you clap your hands the sound comes out without hesitation, and when the moon rises the water doesn't wait to reflect it—it reflects it instantly.

So that instant reflection—and it is also a kind of resonance—is what is looked for as a response of the individual to their environment. And one does this to the degree that they know themselves to be one with their environment. Then this capacity for response increases according to the way in which one feels that they are simply all of a piece with it, and not something that is *in it*, with a barrier around them through which messages have to travel, and that decisions have to be made up and sent out. So you could say that a kind of extremely subtle sensory awareness has to be developed, as between the individual and their environment, so that they can feel it out.

Now today, this sort of talk is very unpopular because scientifically minded people, especially academic scientists teaching in universities, are exceedingly suspicious of intuitive reactions. They say, "You can get into all sorts of trouble that way!" But the thing that they neglect to recognize is that everybody uses it. Even the most meticulously careful, analytical, and rigorously sound scientist uses intuitive judgment after a certain point. Why? Because you may accumulate data forever, and decide that taking all due things into consideration, and procedures having been worked out, that on the whole this is the right thing to do. But why do you decide then? Mostly because time is up, and somebody's pressing for a decision. Or else, you are bored to death with bringing in data, because you never know how much data you need to make a certain decision, and therefore you may go on collecting data till all is blue. But in the last analysis you will work on hunch.

You know, the computer gives you these results and you look them over, and say, "Well, let's flip a coin." So much is actually, in the end, decided by flipping coins. And the pity of flipping coins for making decisions is that it gives you only two choices: heads or tails, one way or the other. The Chinese have a more subtle way of flipping coins: they have a method with a sixty-four-sided coin to flip, so that instead of just heads or tails there are sixty-four possibilities of coming to a decision when you don't know what to do. This is called the *I Ching* (or the *Book of Changes*), where the symbols of *yang* and *yin*—that is to say, for *yang*, a straight line undivided; for *yin*, a line broken in the middle—there are sixty-four ways of combining six of these lines in a hexagram. And so when you have to make a grave decision, there is a complex method for tossing; you do it by tossing sticks or coins, and it gives you one of these sixty-four figures.

Now, if you are very wise and have studied the *Book of Changes* for a long time, you don't need to use the book—you just look at what the figure is and can tell what it means. Because you see, each six-hexagram figure is made up of two three-fold components. For example, you might get a figure that has the two components of water and heaven, so you will have water over heaven. And a person very skilled in the interpretation will feel out the meaning of "water over heaven." But actually, if you're not so skilled, there is the book. And for each of these hexagrams, the book has an oracle which tells you in curiously vague and yet curiously precise terms, the meaning of the hexagram. And then you, in the light of your own situation, make up your mind what it's saying to you—in the light of the problem that you've raised, the question that you've asked, the decision that you had to make. You will find, invariably, that one of these sixty-four choices—or indeed, all of them—has some peculiarly appropriate thing to say to you under your circumstances, just like if you were having a conversation with a very, very wise old gentleman. But you have to pick one of the hexagrams, because after all, you are tossing a coin.

And you must realize that, today in Asia, this book is still widely used for making business and political decisions; although people who are Westernized wouldn't let on, perhaps, that they use it. And so anybody who does politics or business with Asia should be completely versed in this book—to know what sort of thinking, what sort of approach might be expected under any circumstances. If you could ever find out what hexagram had fallen when a certain politician had made a decision, it would be immensely enlightening as to his future course of action.

In the same way, for example, in dealing with Hitler our strategists should have become students of astrology, because he was always consulting astrologers; and therefore, astrology would be much easier to penetrate than the *I Ching* because Hitler was constantly looking at his own horoscope. Well, we have access to Hitler's horoscope—so we know what he was thinking about it. But you don't have access to what hexagram Mao Zedong threw when he decided to do something or other, so it's a little bit more subtle.

Getting back to the point I was making, while our scientists are very suspicious of the intuitive judgment, nevertheless they all use it, in the end. And so this suspicion that science has of intuitive judgment has filtered down to the average person in terms of a mistrust of their own intuition—that is to say, of the marvelous analytical powers of their own brain. And so we are always in a dither of doubt as to whether we are behaving *the right way*, doing *the right thing*, so on and so forth, and lack a certain kind of self-confidence. And if you lack self-confidence, you will make mistakes through sheer fumbling. However, if you do have self-confidence, you may get away with doing the entirely wrong thing.

The British have an enormous degree of self-confidence. They *know* they are right, and they don't even question it. There are certain kinds of British types who are absolutely convinced, and their aplomb is unbelievable. And you can't shake them—they're not even defending themselves they know they're so right. And therefore, they can allow any kind of political revolution, total free speech, and all sorts of things can go on, which make Americans very nervous—because Americans don't have the same degree of aplomb. They're not quite sure, you see? When you're an aristocrat and you've been brought up for generations in the right schools, there is never any doubt whatsoever, you don't even have to mention the fact that you're an aristocrat. That's why aristocrats act as if they know how to treat servants. They never have to emphasize their own superiority because they know they are superior—they don't even question it. Well, this is an extraordinary kind of nerve that they've built up.

Now to do this in Zen practice, first of all, the thing that you have to understand is this: you have to regard yourself as a cloud, in the flesh. Because you see, clouds never make mistakes. Did you ever see a cloud that was misshapen? Did you ever see a badly designed wave?

No, they always do the right thing. Now, as a matter of fact, so do we. Because we are natural beings, just like clouds and waves—only we play complicated games which cause us to doubt ourselves. But if you will treat yourself for a while as a cloud or wave, you will realize that you can't make a mistake—whatever you do. Because even if you do something that seems to be totally disastrous, it will all come out in the wash somehow or other. Then, through this capacity, you will develop a kind of confidence, and through confidence you will be able to trust your own intuition.

Only, the thing that you have to be careful about—and many people who have not understood Zen properly fall into trouble here—is that when they take the attitude that *I can't possibly make a mistake*, they overdo it, which shows that they don't really believe it. So a lot of people come on, and say, "Well, in Zen, anything goes. You are naturally with it anyway. You are a Buddha anyhow. And I'm going to prove I'm a Buddha anyhow, by breaking all the rules." And so you put on the weirdest, filthiest clothes, and you go and steal things, and do things like that. That's overdoing it. That shows that you haven't learned; you're overcompensating. Because you were once told to do this, to do that and the other, and watch and be self-conscious, and nervous, and so on—so you just go to the other extreme.

But there is a middle way—of knowing it has nothing to do with your decision to do this or not. Whether you decide that you can't make a mistake or whether you don't decide it, it's true anyway that you are like cloud and water. And through that realization—without overcompensating in the other direction—you will come to the point where you begin to be on good terms with your own being, and to be able to trust your own brain.

PART THREE

The Watercourse Way

CHAPTER SEVEN

WISDOM OF THE RIDICULOUS

During the previous sessions, I've been talking to you principally about the philosophy of the Lao-tzu book, the *Tao Te Ching*, and now I want to shift today over to Chuang-tzu. This Chuang-tzu, so far as we know, lived about 300 BCE—maybe a little earlier than that—and he is a very, very remarkable person. His book, sometimes simply called the *Chuang-tzu* book, is quite unique in the whole history of philosophy, because he's almost the only philosopher from the whole of antiquity who has real humor; and therefore, he is an immensely encouraging person to read.

But part of his humor is the art of exaggeration—and you always have to allow for that. You always have to realize that he is slightly pulling his own leg. His humor resembles that of a group of enthusiasts who, when talking amongst themselves, carry their own ideas to ludicrous extremes, and roar with laughter about it. And Chuang-tzu does that. Now, for example, he has a great deal to say about the value of the useless life. The whole notion of any moment or event in life being useful—that is to say, serving the end of some future event in life—is absurd to a Taoist. Because nothing is useful in the end. The universe is viewed as purposeless and useless, through and through—because it's a game; although "game" doesn't really convey the sense of this at all.

When a Taoist sage is wandering through the forest he isn't going anywhere; he is just wandering. When he watches the clouds, he loves them because they have no special destination. When he watches birds moving around, or the waves lapping on the shore, he admires them because all this is not busy in the way that human beings are busy—because it serves no end other than being what it is now. And it is for that reason that you get the peculiar styles of Chinese painting in the T'ang, Sung, and later dynasties, where nature, in its wayward wandering nature, is the main subject.

When we say that something is "without purpose" that's a put-down phrase, and when we say, "Well, there is no future in it; what's the use?," we need to realize that these questions reflect our insanity. What's the future in it? What's the use? The joy, for the Taoist, is that things have no use, and the future is not important. Now, you can exaggerate this, and Chuang-tzu does in a very humorous way by describing the ideal, useless man. He's a hunchback, and he is so deformed that his chin rests on his navel. But Chuang-tzu says this man is very admirable, he has found the secret of life. Because when the social service workers come around, he's the first to get a free handout, and when the military officers come around to conscript people for the army, he's the first to be rejected; therefore, he lives long.

Chuang-tzu also describes a case of some travelers who came across an enormous tree—a fantastic thing. And they said, "Never did anyone see such a tree!" So they went up, and looked at it. And first they tested the leaves, but found that they were rough and disagreeable, and no good to eat. Then they looked at the branches, and found that they were all twisted and absolutely no good for using as sticks. Then they examined the wood, and found it was full of pith and absolutely useless for a carpenter. So nobody had disturbed this tree; it was not cut down, or used for any purpose whatsoever; and so it grew to an enormous size and was of great age. Now Chuang-tzu is not exactly asking us to take all that literally. He is pulling our legs here, which is his way of doing things. Then also, he describes the behavior of the highest form of man, and he says:

> The man of character lives at home without exercising his mind, and performs actions without worry. The notions of right and wrong, and the praise and blame of others do not disturb him. When within the four seas all people can enjoy themselves, that is happiness for him. When all people are well provided, that is peace for him. Sorrowful in countenance, he looks like a baby who has lost its mother; appearing stupid, he goes about like one who has lost his way. He has plenty of money to spend, and does not know where it comes from. He drinks and eats just enough, and does not know where the food comes from. This is the demeanor of the man of character. [1]

Then, by contrast, he says:

> The hypocrites are those people who regard as good whatever the world acclaims as good, and regard as right whatever the world acclaims as right. When you tell them that they are men of Tao, then their countenances change with satisfaction. When you call them hypocrites, then they look displeased. All their lives they call themselves "men of Tao," and all their lives they remain hypocrites. They know how to give a good speech and tell appropriate anecdotes in order to attract a crowd. But from the very beginning to the very end, they do

not know what it's all about. They put on the proper garb, and dress in the proper colors, and put on a decorous appearance in order to make themselves popular, but refuse to admit that they are hypocrites.

But this explanation of the man who is stupid in countenance and appearance, and is wandering about as if he had lost his way and doesn't know anything, is of course, based on the text of Lao-tzu, where he says:

The people of the world are merrymaking,
  As if partaking of the sacrificial feasts,
  As if mounting the terrace in spring;
I alone am mild, like one unemployed,
Like a newborn babe that cannot yet smile,
Unattached, like one without a home.

The people of the world have enough and
  to spare,
But I am like one left out,
  My heart must be that of a fool,
  Being muddled, nebulous.

The vulgar are knowing, luminous;
  I alone am dull, confused.
The vulgar are clever, self-assured;
  I alone, depressed.
Patient as the sea,
  Adrift, seemingly aimless.

The people of the world all have a purpose;
I alone appear stubborn and uncouth.
I alone differ from the other people,
And value drawing sustenance from the Mother.[2]

So you see, the character of the Taoist sage, as depicted by Chuang-tzu, is something of the fool. Because the fool is the person who doesn't know enough to come in out of the rain, who doesn't compete. Everybody else gets to the material prizes of life before him, and even to the spiritual prizes. The fool is the person who isn't going anywhere, who isn't interested in survival. He remains the most wonderfully friendly, swinging kind of a character, but he has no ambition; he does not fight for himself, and nobody can ever get him to. So the fool has always been used as a kind of analog of the sage. There is a Hindu verse which says:

Sometimes naked, sometimes mad,
Now as a scholar, now as a fool.
Thus, they appear on earth, the free men.

And if you read the biographies of the early life of Sri Ramakrishna or Sri Ramana Maharshi, they are absolutely wild. But just as in reading Chuang-tzu, you must not take it too literally; these things are said by way of a kind of overstress to correct another kind of overstress in the opposite direction.

Many years ago, when a Japanese scholar explained the teachings of Buddhism to me, he said something I had never heard anybody else say: that the Buddha taught that life is suffering in order to correct the wrong view that it ought to be pleasure. He also said that everything is impermanent in order to correct the wrong view that reality lasts forever in time. So the idea of the Middle Way is set up in this fashion—by going to one extreme in order to correct another.

And this is a very common Eastern technique—found especially in Zen—where, when teachers are asked about something sacred, will always answer in terms of something secular. When asked, "What is the Buddha?," they might answer, "The tree in the garden." Then when you ask about something secular, they answer in terms of something sacred. For example, there's a master and his student working in the field, and they are using a knife to prune, and the student suddenly says to the master, "Give me the knife." And the master gives it to him point first. And so the student says, "But please, let me have the other end." The teacher says, "What would you do with the other end?" You see, the question immediately turns into a kind of a metaphysical thing. So this play, back and forth between the extremes, has as its interior design, the awakening of the mind to polarity—to mutual arising.

Chuang-tzu tells a story about this play. He says, a certain keeper of monkeys, said with regard to their ration of nuts, that each monkey should have three in the morning and four at night. But at this, the monkeys were very angry. So the keeper said they might have four in the morning and three at night, with which arrangement they were all pleased. Now, the number of nuts was the same, he goes on to say, but there was an adaptation to the likes and dislikes of those concerned. This, then he says, is the way of conduct of the sage.

Fundamentally then, Chuang-tzu's philosophy is a philosophy of relativity. There is no absolute standard of great or small, of important or unimportant. There is a story of a sort of *enfant terrible* at a banquet, and when the speeches are being made after dinner, somebody gets up and says that the human being is the highest of all creatures—that the whole world serves humanity. (Which is a lot of pompous nonsense.)

And a small boy gets up and says that since tigers feed on human beings, it's quite obvious, therefore, that human beings exist for the service of tigers. For Chuang-tzu you must get the point of view that small things are as big as big things can be, and big things are as small as small things can be. Everything can be looked at as great or small, important and unimportant—and all the steps between—because his conception of the world is essentially cyclic.

Taoist and Zen teachers have a whole method of teaching with circles. And in drawing circles, the center of a circle is any point on the circumference. Where do you start? You can begin anywhere. The circle of life, the cycle of life, the interdependence of the bees and the flowers, the interdependence of long and short—it's all circular. So there is nowhere, and there is everywhere, that it can begin. In the same way, when Chuang-tzu discusses the organs of the body, he makes a catalog of all these organs and says, "Now, which do you prefer? Which one comes first, and which one follows? Which one rules, and which ones are servants?" He said, it seems that there may be a governor in all this, but nobody could ever find it.

There is an expression, *ch'ien-jan*, which has almost the same meaning as *tzu-jan* (spontaneity, of itself so). *Ch'ien-jan* means "something is so through the power of heaven." Now, heaven (*ch'ien*) means simply "the universe." As you look out from Earth—which is, as it were, the center or the base—everything else, the whole expanse of the cosmos, is *ch'ien* (heaven). There is no connection in this idea of heaven with some sort of personal ruler of the universe. So the notion of God—as we understand it—is really very foreign, indeed, to Taoist thought.

And when you see somebody translating this as "God," it gives a very wrong impression of this teaching. For example, there is a passage in which a student asks a master, "Can one get the Tao so as to have it for one's own?" And the sage answers, "Your body is not your own, it is the delegated image of *ch'ien*"; and missionaries translate that as "God," because they have read in the Bible, "man is made in the image of God." But the master says:

> Your life is not your own, it is the delegated adaptability of heaven. Your offspring are not your own, they are the delegated seeds of heaven. You move, you know not how; you are at rest, you know not why. These are the operations of the ways of Tao.

In accord with the spontaneous rhythm of the universe—that's really what *ch'ien* means.

There isn't even an idea of "the law of nature" in Chinese thought, as we have it. The motions of the body, the harmony of the organism, is not what it is in obedience to a law. So there is no notion in the Taoist philosophy of the world as responding to a boss. So the body does not have a ruling organ in it. Its order is the consequence of, or the operation of, every part of it existing together simultaneously—arising mutually. There is no governor. Now, in Chuang-tzu's philosophy, the difficulty with human beings is they begin to think in terms of governing and ruling, and they set out to dominate themselves and their surroundings. And invariably, this leads to a mess. So, the whole principle then, is one of success in life through *not* pushing it around—through *not* trying to govern it.

As a matter of fact, Chuang-tzu has a very funny trick: a lot of his wisdom he puts into the mouth of Confucius. And he said Confucius was one day doing something and he ran into Lao-tzu, and they had an argument and Lao-tzu won. But then, the next time, he talks about Confucius teaching Lao-tzu's doctrines, and it's to the immense confusion of everybody. But it's said that one day Confucius was standing by a river where there was a tremendous cataract plunging down, and he suddenly saw an old man coming out of the forest who fell into the river, and suddenly disappeared into the cataract. And he said, "Oh dear, too bad! Probably some old fellow tired of life who wanted to put an end to it all."

The next moment, way down stream, the old man pops up out of the water and starts bouncing along. And Confucius is amazed, so he sends one of his disciples to catch this fellow before he disappears. On meeting him, he said, "Sir, I was thinking that you were going to commit suicide, and I suddenly find that you came out of that cataract alive. Do you have some special method by which you do this?"

"No, I have no special method," said the old man. "I just go in with a whirl and come out with a swirl—because I don't resist the water. I entirely identify myself with water."

So here is this old man, utterly relaxed, just rolling around in the torrent and not resisting in any way—and so he is preserved. He goes with the stream, rolls with a punch, or whatever you want to call it. Again, of course, there is exaggeration in a story of this kind—just as there is exaggeration in the story of the hunchback, the tree, and so on. Because true *wu-wei* (or letting go, non-interference) does not mean, for example, flabbiness. A lot of people, when they think they are relaxing, merely become flabby. And if that is so, the perfectly relaxed person would slowly become Jell-O, would spread out on the floor, and finally drip through into the basement.

Relaxation, you see, is simply something that happens when there's too much *yang* in you—too much of the positive. You need to balance off with the *yin*. And the trouble is that human beings, in their anxiety to control things, exhibit too much *yang*—too much aggressiveness, too much of the male principle. They need the balance of the female. And so all these exaggerations in the direction of "let things go," "let things happen," "don't interfere" are stressing the *yin* point of view to compensate for the excess of *yang*.

I remember reading a book called *You Must Relax*. The difficulty always arises when one feels *I must relax*, *I've got to let go and let things happen*. But how on earth do I do it? Even in trying to relax, I'm all tense because I'm anxious that it must happen—and maybe it won't. But you can't achieve *wu-wei* like that. What you have to understand is that you don't have to do anything. There is no method, as the old man said.

When you call the Tao *wu-tse* (or lawless), it means there is no method in it; it's all based on understanding, or what our psychologists call *insight*. You have to find out that there is nothing that you do as a source and cause of action separate from everything else. When you know that—that there is no separate acting "you"—then there is no need to try to relax. The thing you have to see is that the flow of the Tao—as I said before with the illustration of the people swimming in a strong stream—that the flow of the Tao goes on anyway. Just like the flow of time, for example, you can't get out of the present moment. You can think about the past and you can think about the future, but since you do that thinking *now*, the present is inescapable.

All right, now the present moment, it has a sense of flow: time is going along; life is going along. Time, actually, clock time is simply a measure of flow, a way of going *tick, tick, tick, tick*—counting the ticks and saying, "Well, we've lived through so many ticks." But nevertheless, real time—as distinct from this ticking thing—is a flowing. And yet it's still. Isn't that fascinating? It moves, but you're always there; it's always now. You never get out of now. And you can feel that—that you can't get out of now, and you never will. Now, realize that what we call *now* is the same thing as Tao. The Tao—the course of things, the eternal now, the presence of God, anything you want to call it—that's now, and you can't get out of it. So there is no need to get with it because you can't get out. That's beautiful! You just relax, and you're there. So that's the principle of flowing.

You can devise all kinds of very clever ways of postponing finding this out. It's terribly simple, but you can say, "Well, this is a very spiritual matter, and I'm an unevolved person and it will take me a great deal of time to realize this in more than an intellectual way." But that's just an excuse for playing your own game, and not finding this out. There are all sorts of elaborate ways of doing that. You can put it off by indulging in the most complicated systems of spiritual culture, and yoga, and so on, and so forth. And that's all right. I have no objection to your putting it off, if that's what you want to do. But actually, it's *always here and now.* Just as you can't get away from now, you can't get out of the Tao.

That's the humor of the whole thing, and that is why Chuang-tzu has this beautiful light touch. He says:

> The heron is white without a daily bath.
> The crow is black without being painted in ink.

And this is the same saying as in Zen:

> In the spring landscape,
> there is nothing superior, nothing inferior.
> Flowering branches grow naturally;
> Some short, some long.

Well they say, "A long thing is the long body of Buddha. A short thing is the short body of Buddha." Chuang-tzu has this to say about it:

> Those who say that they would have right without its correlate wrong, or good government without its correlate misrule, do

> not apprehend the great principles of the universe, nor the nature of all creation. One might as well talk of the existence of heaven without that of Earth, or of the negative principle, yin, without the positive, yang, which is clearly impossible. Yet people keep on discussing it without stop. Such people must be either fools or knaves.

And of course, one could always reply to Chuang-tzu that there have to be fools and knaves so that we can recognize the existence of sages! He says as much in another way here:

> Speech is not mere blowing of breath, it is intended to say something, only what it is intended to say cannot yet be determined. Is there speech indeed, or is there not? Can we, or can we not, distinguish it from the chirping of young birds?
>
> How can Tao be so obscured that there should be a distinction of true and false? How can speech be so obscured that there should be a distinction of right and wrong? Where can you go and find Tao not to exist? The Tao is obscured by our inadequate understanding, and words are obscured by flowery expressions.
>
> There is nothing which is not this, there is nothing which is not that. What cannot be seen by "that" [the other person] can be known by myself; hence, I say, "this" emanates from "that"; "that" also derives from "this." This is the theory of the interdependence of "this" and "that." Nevertheless, life arises from death, and vice versa. Possibility arises from impossibility, and vice versa. Affirmation is based upon denial, and vice versa.

> Which being the case, the true sage rejects all distinctions and takes his refuge in heaven [that is, in the universe].
>
> For one may base it on this, yet this is also that, and that is also this. This also has its right and wrong, and that has its right and wrong; does then, the distinction between this and that really exist or not? When this, the subjective, and that, the objective, are both without their correlates, that is the very axis of Tao. And when that axis passes through the center—at which all infinities converge—affirmations and denials alike blend into the Infinite One.

You see, the axis of the opposites is the perception of their polarity. The difference between them is explicit, but the unity of them is implicit. There is the explicit difference between two ends of a stick, and the implicit unity that they are ends of the same stick. So that's the axis—the axis of Tao. You might call it "the secret conspiracy"—which is implicit, esoteric, or whatever you want to call it—that it lies between all poles and all opposites, that they are fundamentally one.

So that unity—whether it's between you and the universe, or whatever polarity you want to take—is not something that has to be brought into being. If one *brings it into being* one assumes that it does not exist. In Zen, that is called "putting legs on a snake" or a "beard on a eunuch"—there is something unnecessary. So it exists; it is always there. And you can see it so vividly, and *almost* put your finger on it, and sense it—if you understand that the movement of the Tao is exactly the same thing as the present moment.

Now, of course, if you try to grab the present moment—and get ready, get ready with your clapper, and say, "Now!"—it's gone. The finer and finer you draw the hairline on the watch, to know exactly when *now* is, you eventually get to the point where you can't see it at all. But if you leave it alone and you don't try to grab the moment as it flies, it's always there. You don't have to mark it, you don't have to put your finger on it, because it's everything that there is. And so, the present moment suddenly expands—and it contains the whole of time: all past, all future, everything. You never have to hold on to it.

CHAPTER EIGHT

WAY BEYOND SEEKING

And now, many of you as members of the Anglo-Saxon Protestant subculture of the United States have been brought up to believe that one should *never* take the line of least resistance—that that would be spineless, lacking in courage, will, effort, and all those peculiarly masculine virtues. And we, indeed, have bred a type of male that shares with some Hispanic cultures the attribute of *machismo*, which is overemphasis of male virtues—on being upstanding and outstanding, instead of understanding and in-standing. And of course, you can't have anything *outstanding* unless there is something *in-standing* to compare it with. Likewise, you couldn't imagine a universe of stars—which are bright, hot points of light—except in a universe which contained emptiness or space; they go together.

The Chinese call these two aspects of existence the *yang*, or positive, and the *yin*, or negative. We, of course, have come to associate the *yang* with the male, and the *yin* with the female. And the females don't like to be called "negative," because it is a bad word when we have a philosophy which is based on accentuating the positive—courtesy of Norman Vincent Peale, *Reader's Digest*, Christian Science, and all that kind of diet that accentuates the positive. But obviously, you don't know what the positive is unless you have the contrast of the negative. And women should not be at all ashamed or put off by being associated with the negative, because in a universe where you have *something*, you cannot have it without the courtesy of *nothing*.

This is absent in Western logic. We think that only something exists; whereas as a matter of fact, existence is a conspiracy between something and nothing to appear as different as possible, and yet to be the same. And you will find that equally true of your back and your front—you have to have both. And I invented the word *goeswith* to describe this relationship. So when you understand that *is* goeswith *isn't*, that the positive goeswith the negative, that existence goeswith nonexistence, therefore, in the same way, life goeswith death, your inside goeswith your outside, and your *self* goeswith your *other*. How would you know that you were acting voluntarily unless there were some things that happened to you involuntarily? What would you know about the difference between what *you're doing* and what's *happening to you* unless you had this contrast? It's fascinating! For example, when you breathe, are you "doing" breathing? Is it something you *do*—like you say, "I walk," "I think," "I talk"—or does breathing *happen* to you?

Well, you can feel it both ways. You can feel it as your action, but after all, it goes on while you're not thinking about it, while you're asleep—and in that sense, it seems to be happening to you. Do you grow your hair, or is that something that happens to you, like the rain? Do you shape your bones in a positive way, or does it happen to you? Is your skeleton *you,* or is it something given to you? Well, ordinarily, we always think of ourselves as a bit different from our bodies. We say, "I *have* a body." We very rarely say, "I *am* a body," because we have a special conception of ourselves as an ego, and this is nothing more than a social convention. You are not, obviously, your opinion of yourself. You are not your image of yourself because your image of yourself contains very little information about you.

Most of you is unconscious. Because consciousness is a scanning device, like radar, which is very limited because it can think only of one thing at a time, and life can't be handled with such a primitive instrument. So most things are handled by what psychologists call the *unconscious*, or what I would prefer to call *unconscious processes*. When you say of something, that "it's unconscious," that doesn't mean that it's dumb or stupid. Actually, it's much smarter than consciousness, because consciousness is so limited that it can handle only one thing at a time. And that's why it takes you such an appallingly long time to get educated—because your eyes have to scan ever so many miles of print, and it's tedious and slow, and the universe doesn't operate that way. The universe isn't strung out in a line—one thing after another. It's everything happening altogether everywhere at once. And that's hard to keep track of, if you want to keep track.

Now there are various theories operating in the world about the basic nature of the universe. Fundamentally, there are three of them: the Western, the Hindu, and the Chinese. The Western theory of the universe, whether it is Judeo-Christian or Islamic (because Muslims are really Westerners), and the modern theory, which is what we will call *scientific naturalism*, are all the same. The Western world looks upon the universe as a mechanism, an artifact. And a Western child, naturally asks the question, "How was I made?"—as if you were something made, like we might make a chair out of wood. But ask yourself the question, What is a tree made of? Is a tree *made* of wood? That's kind of a stupid idea. A tree *is* wood; it isn't *made of wood*. A tree grows, it isn't made. There's a difference. And so, if you ask yourself, "How was I made?" you are implicitly defining yourself as a machine. And so, naturally, in psychology we speak of *unconscious mental mechanisms*—looking upon ourselves as a form of machinery explained by psycho-hydraulics according to the principles of Newtonian mechanics.

Now a Hindu does not think of the world as being *made*. A Hindu thinks of the world as being *acted*. And not of God as the original maker, but of God as the actor of all the parts—so that every one of you is a mask which the Godhead is wearing, pretending to be you, and forgetting who He (or rather, She/It) is really. Everybody is God in disguise, playing a game of self-forgetfulness in order that the universe shall not be boring. Because after all, if *you* were God Almighty—and always knew everything, could predict everything, and were in control of everything—such an existence would be like making love to a plastic woman. Not very interesting.

So therefore, it is as important to have a good *forgettory* as it is to have a good memory. And so therefore, every so often, according to the Hindu theory, God forgets Himself (or Itself) and becomes you—with all your problems and limitations—because that's fun. In Sanskrit, it's called *maya*, the "world illusion." The word *maya* also means "magic," and it also means "creation," "creative power"—as we say of an artistic person, a musician, or a poet, that they are creative.

Then there is a third theory—which isn't in conflict with the second, although it is rather in conflict with the first—and that is the world not as an artifact, not as a drama, but as an *organism*. And what on earth is an organism? It's very difficult to define, because an organism grows, and it isn't made. You can tell the difference. When you make something, you assemble parts, or you take a block of wood and cut it into a certain shape by taking pieces away. But watch an organism: it starts as a little seed, and it swells—and as it swells, it complicates itself from the inside outwards; whereas a machine, being put together, comes from outside inwards. And so when you grew out of your mother, you were organized, rather than manufactured.

However, watch out when we say, "Let's get things organized" and talk about a corporation or a political state as *an organization*. They are not really organizations at all because all corporations and political states are based on writing and talk; they're based on laws and procedures that are written down; and therefore, are less intelligent than true, natural organisms, which regulate themselves without having to talk. In other words, your brain is more intelligent than your mind—because your brain can handle more variables than your mind can handle. And by *mind*, I mean your system of thinking, your language, your mathematics, your laws. They're very cumbersome. And as any lawyer knows, it takes forever to understand anything, and you have to go to court and argue it all out, and go on, and on, and on interminably.

Whereas every day your brain handles the entire complexity of getting going in the morning, and getting all your waking and conscious processes operating—your glands, your circulation, your digestion—and it doesn't have to think about it at all. So as every neurologist knows, the brain is smarter than the neurologist because he can't figure it out. He says it's too complicated, but it's not really. What is complicated is the problem of translating what the brain does into language—that's like trying to move the Pacific Ocean into the Atlantic with a fork—it's too slow.

So therefore, the organic view of the universe is that the wisdom of the universe consists in some principle that we cannot really figure out. And one Chinese word for this principle, *li*, means "the markings in jade," "the grain in wood," "the fiber in muscle," "the shapes of clouds," or better yet, "patterns in water." And really, everything is founded on patterns in water. Your body is at least ninety percent water, and therefore everything about you follows patterns characteristic of the flow of water. The fiber in your muscles, your veins, are just like rivers; your bones even, are sculpture commemorating the flow of liquid. So is wood, so is rock: look at the patterns in marble. Air and fire, likewise, follow water patterns, or what we will call the *pattern of flow*. And the flow of the world is really what the Chinese mean by the word *Tao*, the course of nature.

Now, Lao-tzu, who lived probably a little before 400 BCE, if he lived at all—because scholars are always doubting whether anybody ever lived, like Jesus—but nevertheless, Lao-tzu wrote a book called the *Tao Te Ching*. *Tao*: the "flow of nature"; *te:* "its power"; *ching* means "book" or "classic." He started out by saying, "The Tao which can be defined, is not the eternal Tao." In other words, you cannot put the course of nature into exact language—just as you can't see your own head, bite your own teeth, kiss your own lips, and so on. Because what you *are* is always more than *what you think* you are. The "you" that you think you are is not you; it's an image of yourself. And added to that image is also something else: a chronic state of muscular tension, which we are all brought up with.

As children, we are given the basic precept of civilization, which is, you are required to do that which will be acceptable only if you do it voluntarily. *Watch it! You must love me. You must love your mother. Thou shalt love the Lord thy God. Thou shalt love thy neighbor as thy self.* And yet nobody can love by effort, and nobody wants to be loved by effort. Do you want your children to love you just because they are dutiful? Do you want your wife or husband to love you because they think they *ought* to? Or do you rather want them to love you because they can't help it? They are hopelessly in love with you—that's much better, isn't it? So nobody wants to be loved on purpose.

So in other words, the Tao of life is not purposeful. Also, it doesn't operate because it *has to*—there is nothing shoving it. In the organic conception of the world there is no boss. The Chinese word for nature, *tzu-jan*, means "what happens of itself," "the spontaneous." And so when you love, you love spontaneously. When you go to sleep, when you digest your food, when you circulate your blood, when you breathe, it happens of itself. So the nature of the Tao—the saying in Lao-tzu's book, *Tao fa tzu-jan*—is that the principle of operation of the Tao is spontaneity; nobody is pushing anyone around. And funnily enough, there is a similar idea in Christian theology. You've heard about the attributes of God, like omniscience, omnipotence, omnipresence, infinitude, eternity. One they never tell you about is called *aseity*. And *ase* is the Latin for "what happens of itself"—it's the same as the Chinese word *tzu-jan*.

So then, the moral of this is, in life always take the line of least resistance. It's called in Chinese, *wu-wei*, and that means literally, "not forcing." You don't force a key in a lock. If there is stiffness and you force it, you will bend the key and make it useless. And so, likewise, the Taoist principle of *wu-wei* is applied to defending oneself against attack in, say, *judo* or *aikido*—where the principle is, that instead of offering violence to anyone who attacks you, you use the violence of that person to bring about their own downfall. Or you might illustrate it by saying it is more sensible to sail than to row. Rowing will exhaust you. Sailing uses the wind, and if you're a skillful sailor, you can tack and go in a direction opposite to the wind—it will get you there. So in all circumstances of life, one has to cultivate sensitivity to go with the grain, go with the stream, and cultivate the line of least resistance.

Now as I said at the beginning, that strikes us WASP types (white Anglo-Saxon Protestants) as spineless. You ought to stand up—fight! So we talk about *the conquest of nature*, *the conquest of space*, and have these great phallic emblems—rockets, you know—that go *BRRRRHGH* at the heavens. *Wowwee!* But we know if we are men, you can't get an erection on purpose; if it doesn't happen, it isn't real. So all nature works beyond the control of the ego. In fact, there is no ego. The ego, as I tried to show you, is a concept. It's like the equator: an imaginary line between yourself and the rest of the world.

So now, when people think then, of *let's live by taking the line of least resistance*, they usually jump to the conclusion that the way to do that is to do everything the way you are *not* supposed to. I mean, here we have social conventions of morality, of etiquette, and so on, and people say, "Let's throw all these conventions to the wind and be spontaneous." So what they do is they imitate their pre-considered notion of barbarous behavior. But people who do that are complete slaves of convention because they're just doing the opposite of what convention says. They are mirror images of it, and therefore very conventional. You can be conventionally stuffy, and square, and straight; or you can be conventionally bohemian, and act like a freak—Jesus or otherwise. And you are still very conventional; you're not free because the free person has to be very, very sensitive, and feel out the flow of their own nature, find out what he or she really wants to do.

Now that's fundamental. *What do you want? Where are you going? What is the flow of feeling inside you?* And if you explore that, you've got quite a job on your hands, because you will find out many extraordinarily and funny things. First of all, you will discover how much there is in the world that you really don't want to have. Although you've all been brought up to think that you must have certain things, because you've been brought up to think that you must be a good consumer. Your primary duty is to consume for a civilization that is, basically, engaged in producing. But a lot of so-called products are not things that anybody in their senses would want. You know, I often look in a gift shop window and I think *there is not one single thing in this shop that I want.* And I don't want a Cadillac, which is an absolutely stupid, toy rocket ship—it's not good transportation. And I don't want what most people consider wealthy circumstances: you know, a ranch-style house in a nice residential area, where you have to drive for miles in order to get to a shop or a laundry, and you can't take a walk because the police will stop you. That's not wealth; it's boredom.

And also, you not only have to figure out what you really want, but you have to get a new sensation of your identity. *Who are you? What are you?* Now, we are all brought up to think that we are strangers in the universe—that we confront life, that it's something "out there"—and we've got to cope with it, and basically, have a very hostile attitude to the external world. But that's obviously a hallucination. Because if I can't realize what my "self" is, unless it be in contrast to something *not* myself, to something "other," then it very rapidly follows that self and other go together—like front and back, or the north and the south pole of a magnet. You can't have one without the other. So you can't have self without other; and therefore, there's a secret conspiracy between self and other—to look as different as possible, but to be identical.

And so you suddenly get the funny feeling that *what happens to you is what you're doing*. This really scares some people—especially if you were brought up in the Bible Belt—because then you suddenly have to announce that you're God. What *happens* to you is what you *do*—and that's a terrible responsibility. Anyway, you are considered crazy if you announce that you're God. It's what happened to Jesus, and they crucified him. If he had lived in India, it would have been quite different because everybody would have said, "Oh splendid! You found out"—because everybody is God in disguise. There would have been no crucifixion. And so I suppose the world wouldn't have been saved; although, it was saved anyway.

To put it, though, into terms that are more acceptable to the scientific temperament of the Western world, we wouldn't say *you are*

God, because that word has mythological associations of a patriarchal authority, based on the Pharaohs of Egypt and the Cyruses of Persia—which is, of course, idolatry. The monarchical image of God is idolatrous in a far more dangerous way than any image made of wood or stone. And that's one of the main reasons for social conflict in the United States: we are a republic, but the citizens of the republic to a large extent believe—or think they *ought* to believe—that the universe is a monarchy. Therefore, they're always talking about *respect for authority* and *law and order*, which is bad form for citizens of a republic.

But the whole idea of a republic is mutual consent—of trusting each other, and not handing over your responsibilities to policemen. Because who guards the guards? Well, the answer is always *you do*. Or as De Tocqueville put it, a people gets what government it deserves. So we cannot avoid responsibility in that sense—there's no way. So therefore, you have to find out what you really want to do. *Which way does your inner incline you to go?* (As George Fox would have called it, your "inward light.")

I have proposed that the new form of college entrance examination be that every student requiring admission to college be asked to write a paper of about twenty pages on his or her idea of heaven—*What would be the happiest possible thing that could happen to you?* Then that paper would be given to a tutor, who reads it over, and says, "Is this what you *really* want? Don't you realize that if you say you want *this*, that it goes with *that*? You said you want this kind of a girl, but you said nothing about her mother, and that goes with her"—and so on and so on, until the entrance examination turns into the doctoral dissertation, having been really carefully thought out. I think it would be a good idea because we don't really explore what we really want.

We take in all sorts of things that we are *told we want*. We take in all kinds of ideas of ourselves that we're told we are. You are told who you are by your parents, and your teachers, and your peers. But they don't know who you are because they don't know who they are. Nobody knows who is who, because the eyes can't look at themselves. So we are all fundamentally mysterious and indefinable—you can't grab yourself. Therefore, you have to trust yourself, and have faith in yourself—faith in your own, what psychologists would call *unconscious*; and also, faith in other people is absolutely fundamental. It's very risky. You can't always rely on it. Mistakes will happen. Things will go apparently wrong. But the alternative to it is the police state, where everything is foolproof and under control. No surprises!

Basic, therefore, to the Chinese view of nature—whether it is what we call *nature outside* (the birds, the bees, and the flowers) or whether it's *human nature*—is that you must trust it. There's no alternative, so *go with it*. It will get you into trouble sometimes, but in the long run it works—because that's what we've always been doing.

Now, not so long ago, there was a meeting of geneticists at the University of California, and the geneticists figured that they were in sight of being able to breed human beings perfectly. By altering the genes, we could get all the desirable character types and eliminate the undesirable ones. So thinking they were about to do this, they summoned a whole bunch of theologians and philosophers and said, "Now, we have this fantastic power. What kind of human beings should we breed?" Well, a lot of hot air was talked, and finally I said, "For heaven's sake, be sure to breed as many different kinds as possible! Because we never know what kind of human beings we're going to need. In one age, we may need cooperative people. In another age, we may need aggressive people. We may need organization men; we may also need mavericks. We don't know what kind of people we will need."

And the reason we don't know is that our verbal wisdom—anything that can be said in words, encoded in laws, or set down in number series (even when being capable of being very rapidly analyzed by computers)—these are systems which nowhere approach the intelligence and the complexity of the system of nature, and therefore don't comprehend it. Verbal systems can do nothing more than make caricatures of the real world, which is what you are.

So the gamble of faith in yourself as identical with the energy field in which you live—otherwise known as the universe—is something you can't avoid any more than you can avoid living in the present. Because whether you think of the past or think of the future, that's all happening *now*—there is nowhere else to be. So, as when Margaret Fuller wrote to Thomas Carlyle a long letter and said at the end of it, "In short, I accept the universe," he commented, "My God, she had better."

Now, when we don't trust the universe, we take a hostile stance. And such an aggressive attitude to nature is very heavily rooted in a belief system, current in this country, which is that active is good and passive is bad. And our very ideas of the active and the passive are unexamined. There is all the difference in the world in the word *active*, between different kinds of being active. When we say of an artistic performance that "it's forced," we mean that a lot of effort went into it, but it was no good. We could see this person straining to do the good thing. I mean, supposing in talking to you I was umming and erring all the time, and frowning, and obviously making an enormous struggle to talk to you, you would say, "This man is a bore!"—and go away, or go to sleep. But in order to keep you interested, I have to pretend that I'm talking off the top of my head, and I really don't know how I'm doing it.

So, there are kinds of energy which are unforced. There may be effort in them, but they are unforced, and so, in a certain sense of the word, passive. I am, in other words, responsive to what Socrates called a *Daimon*. He had a demon in himself—a good demon. There are good demons and bad demons, but anyway, there's a demon who turns me on, and I don't know how it happens. There's a Japanese poem which says, "If you want to know where the flowers come from, even the God of spring doesn't know." And that's why we can't teach music. We can teach the technique of music, the notation, how to put your fingers on the keys, but that doesn't teach the person what music to make. If a person has music inside, then the technique can be used to express it, but if you've got no music in you, all you'll do is just play exercises.

It's quite natural that many places outside America and the Western world—like Asia, Africa, the Middle East, and so forth—are adopting the Western mechanistic model of the universe. They've been so impressed by the achievements of Western civilization that they want to jump on the bandwagon just at the moment when we are becoming rather disillusioned with it all. But we cannot renounce technology. Millions would starve without the achievements of modern technology. So what we've got to do, somehow, is to figure out a way of using technology which is not ecologically disastrous—and that's a very skillful problem. There are people who are studying this, and know a great deal about it, how to flow with the course of nature, but be intelligent about it—technologically intelligent. It can be done.

After all, sailing is technology, and as Buckminster Fuller has pointed out, sailors were probably the fundamental originators of civilization. But sailing is based on *going with* the wind (and the currents), and on navigation, observing the stars. So it's an entirely intelligent operation. Lots of birds navigate by the stars. White throats, for example, migrate by celestial navigation. And so this is a kind of *cooperative technology*, as distinct from *hostile technology*—the technology of the bulldozer, wherein hideous fulfillment of Isaiah's prophecy, every valley shall be exalted, and every mountain laid low, and the rough places made plain. For, you know, make straight in the desert, a highway for our God, the automobile, which is being done all over California and everywhere else. And that's a colossal parody.

Let's go back into the politics of this. One of the political groups, which along with the Quakers and the Anabaptists, who were the founders of Democratic ideas in the 17th century, was known as the Levellers. And the idea of the Levellers, which is misinterpreted, is that everybody be made equally inferior. It's a parody of democracy to say *you're all equally inferior*—and that wasn't the original idea at all. The idea of the Levellers is that all of you are incarnations of God—*you're all equally superior*—equally apertures through which the universe is aware of itself.

Therefore, when a Hindu greets you, instead of shaking hands (which means "no sword") he bows; he reverences the Godhead in you by saying, "Namaste." Of course, it becomes a superficial social custom, but I notice it being taken on increasingly in this country—especially around colleges and with young people, where they have a sense of the real value, the "You," in the other. I am also a "You." You are just as much I as I am, and "I" is the name of God: *Yahweh*. When Jesus said, "Before Abraham was, I Am," he understood.

CHAPTER NINE

WISDOM OF THE WATERCOURSE

I'm going to talk to you about Taoism, which is one of the principal forms of Chinese philosophy, as it were, the opposite number of Confucianism—for these two ways of thought lie at the roots of Chinese civilization. So now, when it comes to Taoism, this is a point of view that becomes explicit in Chinese history in the neighborhood of 400 BCE, and the book is called the *Tao Te Ching*. *Tao* is usually translated "the Way," but I would prefer to call it "the course"—"the course of nature." And *te* means "virtue," but in the sense that we use the word *virtue* when we say, "the healing virtue of a plant." It has a magical connotation, or a connotation of power and peculiar skill.

So then, I want to discuss a few of the main ideas of Lao-tzu, and naturally, we start with Tao. This word in Chinese is connected with motion—going on and stopping, or rhythmic motion (on and off)—and this other part of the character here means intelligence. So you've got "intelligent motion," "the course of nature." So you have in the idea of Tao, the flow of life, the flow of events, the world considered as a stream. And water is very often used by Lao-tzu to give the idea of Tao, because water always takes the line of least resistance. Water is very soft, and yet is one of the strongest things in the world; you can chop water with a sword, but leave no wound; you can't squeeze it; you can't compress it. Tao is always gentle, always yielding; it is feminine, in this way.

Lao-tzu says, "Although you may be male, always have a certain bit of the feminine, and thus you will become a universal channel." That has particularly to be learned by men in the United States, who tend to overcompensate masculinity—and to be ashamed of gentleness. As a result, we have a lot of misunderstanding between men and women, because each one is so busy being their particular sex that they have nothing in common. So in this idea then, is the strength of gentleness.

And of course, it is ultimately on this philosophy that the Japanese worked out the science of *judo*, "the gentle way"—whereby a strong man is alarmingly defeated by the use of his own strength against himself. And the analogy is, of course, of the pine tree and the willow tree. The pine tree is a muscle man, and when the snow piles up, and piles up, and becomes icy, the pine tree branch cracks. But when the willow has snow piling on it, after a little while the branch drops, the snow falls off, and the branch swings up again—that's *judo*. In Japan, they teach a mysterious science called *aikido*—again, *do* meaning Tao. *Aikido* is the inner, or esoteric, aspect of *judo*. And they can teach you, for example, to hold out your arm in such a way that no one can bend it—however strong. But it all depends on your not using effort to hold it out; you must not resist. There is a certain way of doing that.

So this Tao cannot be defined—that's basic. Just because it is the flow of nature, you can't capture it. You can't shut up wind in a box, and expect it to be wind. You can't catch flowing water in a bucket because the minute it's in the bucket, it's no longer flowing.

Now Tao, then, means roughly what we would mean by the basic energy of the world. But there are two things to be said about it, and the first is that it is not a governing energy. Here we clearly come up against the principle, or a concept, of nature in which there is no government. This is an anarchic view of the universe—not in the sense of chaos, but equally, not in the sense of what we seem to mean by order. The Tao does not rule. Lao-tzu says:

> The great Tao flows everywhere,
>   both to the left and to the right,
> It loves and nourishes all things,
>   but does not lord it over them.
> And when merits are accomplished,
>   it lays no claim to them.

In fact, the Tao is always self-effacing—always disappears, and is always indefinable, always behind the scenes. And so, in a way, the Lao-tzu book is written as a manual of advice to rulers, and his idea of a good ruler is one who is never in evidence. Do you know, for example, the name of your sanitation chief? I bet you don't. But he is a very, very important official. And Lao-tzu would advise the President of the United States to behave like the chief of sanitation: to be unobtrusive, and to generally leave things alone—let things take their course.

We think in the West that the order of nature has a plan underneath it—that there was, as it were, the original blueprint in the mind of God, which is the Logos (the second person of the Trinity). But the Chinese don't think that way. They would tend to agree with the humor of the limerick:

> There was a young man who said, "Damn.
> For it certainly seems that I am,

a creature that moves in determinate grooves.
I'm not even a bus, I'm a tram."

But the Chinese do not think of any rails laid down, as it were, or rules laid down, upon which nature has to travel. They think simply that it organizes itself, but doesn't know how. It's just like a centipede, which manages one hundred legs without thinking—because thinking would embarrass it. That sort of thing is called, in Chinese, "putting legs on a snake." A snake needs no legs, so explaining the universe by a governor that dominates it, is called "legs on a snake."

It's like saying, we have an instinct to do this, that, and the other. When people talk about instincts, watch out—they are invoking ghosts. When we say we have "an instinct to survive," it means simply that we do survive, in fact, until we don't. And if you want to explain the curious fact that people seem to want to survive, you call it an instinct to survive—and this is learned gobbledygook. There was a time when you showed a physician or a scientist some peculiar thing which he did not understand, and he would put on his spectacles, examine it from various points of view, make a few notes, and then say, "It is *lusus naturae*." And everybody would say, "Wonderful! He knows what it is: *lusus naturae*." But all that means is it's a game of nature, a freak. And you will find that many, many medical people practice this sort of gobbledygook. For example, when you have a pain, they say *it's neuritis*—which simply means that your nerves hurt. So, it's always good to translate medical language back into English, and you begin to get some idea of what's happening.

Now the next thing to take up is the word *te*, and as I said, this means "virtue," "power," and sometimes "magic." When we say a person is a virtuoso, we have something of the meaning of *te* in it—marvelous accomplishment. And in opening the section on *te*, Lao-tzu says:

Superior virtue is not virtue,
and thus is virtue.
Inferior virtue cannot let go of virtue,
and thus is not virtue.

Or we might say, a person who really has virtue is not striving for virtue—and thus really has it. A person of inferior virtue is so trying to be virtuous that they are not virtuous. In other words, when the person is trying and striving for virtue, they are being self-conscious and artificial. And we say, "Well, so-and-so is very good, but isn't he rather forced? Isn't he a bit phony?" And it's so often the case that people who are reputedly very virtuous are very boring. You feel that sometimes people are so good that you are sitting on the edge of your chair in their presence, and that you cannot relax with them, or let your hair down because they are full of judgment and disapproval—because they are always judging and disapproving of themselves. A really virtuous person doesn't show their virtue—like the Chinese poem which says:

Entering the forest,
he doesn't disturb a blade of grass.
Entering the water,
he doesn't make a ripple.

He looks very ordinary, and so his virtue cannot be detected, and so it is said he doesn't stink of virtue.

So *te*, then, is the virtue of the great artist or craftsman, who creates marvelous works of art, but always as if making no effort. And so we say of great art, that *it's artless*—that it seems to come naturally, that the artist does it as if they were falling off a log. Now, of course, we know that it isn't that simple; but nevertheless, it does seem to be so. And what everybody wants to know, is how to acquire that great naturalness—in everything—so that we in our human lives manifest the Tao. Tao manifested through man is *te*.

How do you do it? So the transitional word, which shows the way to realize *te* in one's life, is *wu-wei*. *Wei* means "to act," "to strain," "to strive," or "to interfere"; and as I said before, *wu* means "non" or "not." And so the Taoist manner of life is *wu-wei*—don't force it. Always go with the stream. You may need to use a rudder, but don't ever go against the stream. If you are swimming and caught in a very strong current, you will be lost if you try to swim against it. You must swim *with it* and edge to the side to escape—that's *wu-wei*.

This has been very well understood even by the samurai in Japan, who, when they became great masters of swordsmanship, always found out and belonged to the No Sword School, because the real master of the sword never uses one. There is a story that in ancient times in Japan, there were two master swordsmiths, and there was a great debate as to which of them was the better. So some soldiers took a sword made by each master, and decided to test them out. They first took a sword made by the man who, in general opinion, was perhaps a little inferior. And they went to a stream, and they dipped the sword in the stream, with the edge of the blade facing upstream, and they dropped a piece of paper on the stream, and it floated towards the sword. And as it floated, the sword simply divided it in two, the two pieces of paper joined together on the other side and went on down the stream. They then took the blade of the man reputed perhaps to be the greatest master, and thought, "Well, it would be pretty difficult to improve on that, but we'll try it anyway." So they gave the same test. But as the piece of paper approached the sword, it moved over to one side, skirted it altogether, and went on. So the true master will never have to be in a fight.

And for that reason, *aikido*, as an athletic technique, is learning how to be unattackable—to always avoid the fight—so that however hard people strike at you they will always be hitting the air. That is *te*, that's magical power. But it all comes about through not using effort, never straining, at anything. Like you never force a key in a lock; you'll just bend the key—instead, you jiggle and jiggle and jiggle, until it turns smoothly. Or you put oil on it, or something to work with it—but never force it. Same way when you use your eyes: don't stare at anything in order to see it clearly, because you'll just tire out your eyes and make the image fuzzy. If you want to see the time on a distant clock, you close your eyes, you imagine black and relax your eyes, then look at the clock, lazily, and you will see that the detail is clearer.

Now there's another story which will exemplify this. Later than Lao-tzu, there was another Taoist sage called Lieh-tzu, and he had the reputation of being able to ride on the wind. (Of course, that's metaphorical.) And so when D.T. Suzuki was asked what it's like to have the experience of satori or enlightenment, he once said, "It is like ordinary everyday experience, except it's about two inches off the ground"—where you don't feel burdened by your own body, where you don't feel you were something that you have to lug about, hold a club over, and generally boss around.

So the sense of lightness, that is the meaning of Lieh-tzu being able to walk on the air. But he told a story of how he managed to do it. He said he went to a great guru, and this guru paid no attention to him, so he just sat outside the door of his hut. And a year went by. And still, this man paid no attention to him. So Lieh-tzu went away, disgusted. But then he thought it over a bit, and realized this man had a terrific reputation, and that if perhaps he had been a little bit more patient, he would have had some teaching. So he went back. And the great sage looked at him and said, "Why this ceaseless coming and going?" So he sat down again at the entrance of the hut, and for a further year, attempted to control his mind in such a way as never to think of profit or loss, or advantage or disadvantage. And then at the end of that year, the teacher looked at him. For another year, he practiced, and at the end of that, the teacher invited him to come in the hut and sit on the mat. Then for the next year, however, he did something quite different. And he says this:

> I let my eyes see whatever they wanted to look at. I let my ears hear whatever they wanted to hear. I let my mouth say whatever it wanted to say. And I let my mind think whatever it wanted to think. And at the end of that year, I didn't know what was "subject" and what was "object." I didn't take any account of time. I was riding on the wind, but I didn't really know whether the wind was riding on me, or I was riding on the wind.

And this was when he got to float, you see. He allowed democracy to prevail. He said to his eyes, "I'm not going to try to control you. You know better how to see than I do." To his ears, "I'm not going to force you to listen to anything. You know how to hear better than I can direct you," and so on for everything. He trusted his own brain; he trusted his own organism. This is *wu-wei.*

So in exactly the same way, if you practice meditation, don't *try* to meditate. Like the choir was told not to try to sing—don't force it. When you meditate, let your lungs breathe the way they want to breathe; let your mind think anything it wants to think about—don't try to repress thoughts. Let your eyes see whatever they're looking at; and let your ears, your eardrums, vibrate to any oscillations there may be in the air. Let go. You may think that's very risky—but it isn't, it really isn't. It's like a ship in a typhoon: they always shut the engines off, and drift. Because if the propellers are going and the tail end of the ship is thrown up so as to be above the water level, the whole ship will vibrate and be shaken to pieces by those revolving propellers. So in a big storm—and life is a big storm all the time—you let go, and you become like a cork on the water, or a ping pong ball in a mountain stream. That is what's called *purposelessness* in Taoism—which is a form of *wu-wei*. And a Taoist text says, "When purpose has been used to achieve purposelessness, the point has been grasped."

So, it's the same problem we have in India, where there's a superstition that if you think of a monkey while you're taking medicine, the medicine won't work. So you are in the predicament of trying not to think of the monkey while taking medicine. And that happens to us whenever we try to be natural—everybody can see that it's forced, it's faked. And so, you think then, "How can I be genuinely natural? How can I *really* flow with the course of nature? How can I let my mind think whatever it wants to think?" Because the moment I start doing that, I realize I am doing it with an ulterior motive; I'm trying to meditate; I'm trying to grow spiritually—and that ruins the whole thing.

Well, when you've tried for a long time to get the right attitude, and you find that all the attitudes you get are phony ones, then you come to the realization that there is nothing you can do about it. It really doesn't make any difference. And again, the principle that I've emphasized all along is you give up—and in so doing, you gain the strength and energy that you were looking for. It's like trying to live in the present.

Gurdjieff used to give his students an exercise that he called "self-remembering"—that is, constantly, all day long being completely aware of what you're doing, having your mind always on the immediate moment. Oh, and it's tough, tough, tough to do that—you get distracted all the time—until one fine day you realize to your astonishment, that there is no way, at all, of having your mind anywhere else *but in the present moment.* Because even when you think about the past or the future, you're doing it now, aren't you? And that results in a very curious transformation of consciousness. You feel the present moment is flowing along and carrying you with it—all the time—just like the flow of the Tao. The flow of the Tao is what we may call *the flow of the present*, and you're with it. There is no way of being anywhere else.

The *Zhongyong*—the book called *The Wobbling Pivot*—says, "The Tao is that from which one cannot deviate; that from which one can deviate is not the Tao." Or to put it into the form of a Zen story:

> Joshu said to Nansen, "What is the Tao?"
> Nansen replied, "Your everyday mind is the Tao."
> Joshu asked, "How do you get into accord with it?"
> Nansen replied, "When you try to accord, you deviate."

So that is the principle, the paradox. This sounds like a completely *laissez-faire*, spineless attitude to life, but it is precisely Taoism, which in common with Buddhism underlies the greatest achievements of Chinese art and culture. It also underlies *judo*, and the Zen arts of Japan—calligraphy, architecture, gardens. It's the form of Chinese philosophy, which in subsequent years became most interested in science and in the study of nature.

The Confucians never had any interest in science because they were bookish people, absorbed in texts. They were essentially scholastics, and never opened the book of nature. But the Taoists were always observing natural phenomena and how they worked. They were interested, above all, in manual skills and using the Tao to perfect manual skills. And therefore, these lazy people achieved the most interesting results, because they were like water, which is lazy, and always seeks the line of least resistance—but that is almost the same thing as intelligence.

PART FOUR

The Line of Least Resistance

CHAPTER TEN

DROPPING OUT FROM KARMA

In India, it is believed, generally, that when a person sets out on the way of liberation, their first problem is to become free from their past *karma*. The word *karma* literally means "action" or "doing" in Sanskrit, so that when we say that something that happens to you is "your karma," it's like saying in English, "It's your own doing." But in popular Indian belief, *karma* is a sort of built-in moral law, or a law of retribution, such that all the bad things you do and all the good things you do have consequences which you have to inherit; and so long as karmic energy remains stored up, you have to work it out.

And what the sage endeavors to do is a kind of action, which in Sanskrit, is called *nishkama karma*. *Nishkama* means "without passion" or "without attachment," and *karma* means "action." And so, whatever action he does, he renounces the fruits of the action—so that he acts in a way that does not generate future karma. Because future karma continues you in the wheel of becoming (i.e., *samsara*, the "round") and keeps you being reincarnated.

Now then, in that case when the time comes that you start to get out of the chain of karma, all the creditors that you have start presenting themselves for payment. In other words, a person who begins on the path of awakening, it's felt that they will suddenly get sick, or that they lose money, or all sorts of catastrophes will occur—because the karmic debt is being cleared up. And it is in no hurry to be cleared up if you're just living along like anybody. But if you embark on the spiritual life, a certain hurry occurs; and therefore, since this is known, it's rather discouraging to start these things.

The Christian way of saying the same thing is that if you plan to change your life—shall we say, "to turn over a new leaf"—you must not let the devil know. Because he will oppose you with all his might if he suddenly discovers that you are going to escape from his power. So, for example, if you have a bad habit—say, you drink too much—and you make a New Year's resolution that during this coming year you will stop drinking. That is a very, very dangerous thing to do because the devil will immediately know about it. And what will happen will be this: he will confront you with the prospect of 365 drinkless days, and that will be awful, you know, just overwhelming, and you won't be able to make much more than three days on the wagon.

So in that case, you compromise with the devil, and say, "Just today, I'm not going to drink. But tomorrow maybe, you know, we'll go back." Then when tomorrow comes, you say, "Oh, just another day, let's try it out—that's all." And the next day you say, "Oh, one more day won't make much difference." So you only do it for the moment, and you don't let the devil know that you have a secret intention of going on day after day after day after day.

But of course, there is something still better than that—and that is not to let the devil know anything. And that means, of course, not letting yourself know. One of the many meanings of that old saying,

"Let not your left hand know what your right hand doeth" is just this. And that was why in Zen discipline, a great deal of it centers around acting without premeditation. As those of you know, who read Eugen Herrigel's book *Zen in the Art of Archery*, it was necessary to release the bow string without first saying "now." And so this is one of the great, great problems in the spiritual life—or whatever you want to call it—which is to be able to have intention and act simultaneous. By this means you escape karma, and you escape the devil.

So, you might say that the Taoist is exemplary in this respect—that this is getting free from karma without making any previous announcement. Supposing we have a train, and we want to unload the train of its freight cars, you can go to the back end and unload them one by one, and shunt them into the siding. But the simplest of all ways of unloading is to uncouple between the engine and the first car—and that gets rid of the whole bunch at once. And it is in that sort of way that the Taoist gets rid of karma without challenging it—so it has the reputation of being "the easy way."

There are all kinds of yogas and ways for people who want to be difficult. One of the great gambits of a man like Gurdjieff was to make it all seem as difficult as possible, because that challenged the vanity of his students. If some teacher, some guru says, "Really, this isn't difficult at all; it's perfectly easy," some people will say, "Oh, he's not really the real thing." We want something tough and difficult, and when we see somebody starts out giving you a discipline that's very, very weird and rigid, people think, "Now *there* is the thing. That man means business!" And so they flatter themselves by going to such a guy—that they are serious students—whereas the other people are only dabblers, and so on. All right, if you have to do it that way, that's the way you have to do it.

But the Taoist is the kind of person who shows you the shortcut, and shows you how to do it by intelligence rather than effort—because that's what it is. Taoism is in that sense, what everybody is looking for: the easy way in, the short cut, using cleverness instead of muscle.

So when the wind blows and one of those thistledown seeds responds like a living animal, you can't say that it's not a living animal—that it's only a seed with whiskers on—because those whiskers on the seed are a manifestation of the intelligence of the seed, in the same way as the sail manifests the intelligence of the sailor. But the question naturally arises: "Isn't it cheating?" When in any game somebody really starts using their intelligence, they will very likely be accused of cheating. Drawing the line between skill and cheating is a very difficult thing to do. The inferior intelligence will always accuse a superior intelligence of cheating—that's its way of saving face. *You beat me by means that weren't fair. We were originally having a contest to prove who had the strongest muscles, but then you introduce some gimmick into it—some judo trick or something like that—and you're not playing fair!*

So in the whole domain of ways of liberation, there are routes for the stupid people and routes for the intelligent people, and the latter are faster. This was perfectly, clearly explained by Hui-neng (the six patriarch of Zen in China), in his sutra, where he says the difference between the gradual school and the sudden school is they both arrive at the same point, but the gradual is for slow-witted people and the sudden is for fast-witted people. Can you, in other words, find a way that sees into your own nature—that sees into the Tao—immediately? In previous talks, I pointed out to you the immediate way—the way through *now.*

When you know that this moment is the Tao, and this moment is considered by itself, without past and without future ... eternal—neither coming into being nor going out of being—there is what is called nirvana. And there is a whole Chinese philosophy of time based on this. It hasn't, to my knowledge, been very much discussed by Taoist writers. It's been more discussed by Buddhist writers, but it's all based on the same thing. Dogen, the great thirteenth-century Japanese Zen Buddhist, studied in China and he wrote a book called *Shobogenzo*. A roshi recently said to me in Japan, "That's a terrible book, because it tells you everything. It gives the whole secret away!" But in the course of this book, he says there is no such thing as a progression in time. "The spring does not become the summer. There is first spring, and then there is summer."

So in the same way, you *now* do not become you *later*. This is T.S. Eliot's idea in *Four Quartets*, where he says that the person who has settled down in the train, to read the newspaper, is not the same person who stepped onto the train from the platform. And therefore, also, you who sit here, are not the same people who came in at the door. These states are separate—each in its own place. There was the coming-in-at-the-door person, but there is actually, only the here-and-now-sitting person. And the person sitting here and now is not the person who will die—because we are all a constant flux.

The continuity of the person from past through present to future is as illusory, in its own way, as the upward movement of the red lines on a revolving barber pole. You know, it goes round and round and round, and the whole thing seems to be going up or going down, whichever the case may be. But actually, nothing is going up or down. So when you throw a pebble into the pond and you make concentric rings of waves, there is an illusion that the water is flowing outwards—but no water is flowing outwards at all. Water is only going up and down. What appears to move outward is the wave, not the water.

So this kind of philosophical argument says that our *seeming to go along in a course of time* does not really happen. The Buddhists say:

> Suffering exists, but no one who suffers.
> Deeds exist, but no doers are found.

A path there is, but no one who follows it.
And Nirvana is, but no one who attains it.

In this way, they look upon the continuity of life as the same sort of illusion that is produced when you take a cigarette and whirl it in the dark, which creates the illusion of a circle.

The argument then is *so long as you're in the present, there aren't any problems; the problems exist only when you allow presents to amalgamate.* There's a way of putting this in Chinese, which is rather interesting. They have a very interesting sign, which is pronounced *nien* (and in Japanese, *nen*); and the top part of the character means "now," and the bottom part means the "mind-heart" (the *hsin*); and so this is, as it were, "an instant of thought." In Sanskrit, they use this character as the equivalent for the Sanskrit word *ksana*. Then if you double this character and put it twice, or three times—*nien, nien, nien*—which means "thought after thought after thought."

Now, the Zen master, Joshu, was once asked, "What is the mind of a child?"

And he said, "A ball in a mountain stream."

"What do you mean by a ball in a mountain stream?"

He said, "thought after thought after thought, with no block." So, he was using, of course, the mind of the child as the innocent mind—the mind of a person who is enlightened—one thought follows another without hesitation. The thought arises; it doesn't wait to arise, as when you clap your hands—the sound issues without hesitation. When you strike flint, the spark comes out—it doesn't wait to come out. And that means that there is no block. So "thought, thought, thought"—*nien, nien, nien*—describes what we call, in our world, *the stream of consciousness*. Blocking consists in letting the stream become connected—chained together—in such a way that when the present thought arises, it seems to be dragging its past or resisting its future, saying, "I don't want to go." When then, the connection (the *dragging*, it's better to call it) of these thoughts drops, you have broken the chain of karma.

Now, if you think of this in comparison with certain problems in music, it's very interesting. Because when we listen to music, we hear melody only because we remember the sequence—we hear the intervals between the tones. But more than that, we remember the tones that led up to the one we are now hearing, and we are trained musically to anticipate certain consequences. And to the extent that we get the consequences we anticipate, we feel that we understand the music. But to the extent that the composer does not adhere to the rules—and gives us unexpected consequences—we feel that we don't understand the music.

And if he gives us harmonic relationship, which we are not trained to accept—that is to say, to expect—we say, "Well, this man is just writing garbage!" But of course, it becomes apparent that the perception of music—the ability to hear melody—will depend upon a relationship between past, present, and future sounds. And you might say, "Well, you're talking about a way of living that would be equivalent to listening to music with a tone-deaf mind so that you would eliminate the melody and have only noise. And so in your Taoist way of life, you would eliminate all meaning and have only senseless present moments." Up to a point, that's true. That is, in a way, what Buddhists also mean by seeing things in their *suchness*.

What is so bad about dying, for example? It's really no problem. When you die, you just drop dead—that's all there is to it. But what makes it a problem is that you're dragging a past. And all those things you've done, all those achievements you've made, all these relationships and people that you've accumulated as your friends, all that has to go. See, it isn't here now. I mean, a few friends might be around you, but all that past that identifies you as who you are—which is simply memory—

all that has to go, and we feel just terrible about that. But if we didn't—if we were just dying, that's all—death wouldn't be a problem.

So in the same way, if you're washing dishes, it's only possible to wash one dish at a time—and that's not very difficult. But when you have a large stack of dishes, you think about all the future dishes you've got to wash while you're washing any one of them; and also, you remember all the many times you've washed dishes in the past. Likewise, the chores of everyday life: they become intolerable when everything ties together—all the past and the future, you feel it dragging at you every way.

Supposing you wake up in the morning and it's a lovely morning. Let's take today, right here and now: here we are in this paradise of a place, Big Sur, and some of us have got to go to work on Monday. Is that a problem? For many people, it is. It spoils the taste of what is going on now. And when we wake up in bed on Monday morning and think of the various hurdles we have got to jump that day, immediately we feel sad and bored and bothered; whereas actually, we're just lying in bed. So the Taoist trick says *simply live now and there will be no problems*. That's the meaning of the Zen saying:

> When you are hungry, eat.
> When you are tired, sleep.
> When you walk, walk.
> When you sit, sit.

Rinzai, the great Tang Dynasty master, said:

> In the practice of Buddhism, there is no place for using effort. Sleep when you're tired, move your bowels, eat when you're hungry. That's all. The ignorant will laugh at me, but the wise will understand.

And so, also, the meaning of this wonderful Zen saying, *tai tai*, every day is a good day—on condition, however, that you don't link them. *Tai, tai* is like *nien, nien*; they come one after another, and yet there is only this one.

This, as I intimated just a moment ago, seems to be an atomization of life. It seems to say, "Well, you shouldn't be carried away by the music; this guy playing the violin is only a scraping cat's entrails with horsehair." Or, "What is there to get excited about in golf? All you're doing is knocking a little ball around with a stick." At a glance it seems to be completely disintegrative, breaking up the continuity of life into point instants, like a calculus. But you must understand that this is not the final state. This is something that's initial, that you learn to do first so that you can later enjoy the illusion. This is to say, this is the way things really are—just suchness. They have no meaning. Things just do what they do. The flower goes *poof*, and people go this way, go that way, and so on—and that's what's happening. It has no meaning; it has no destination; it has no value—it's just like *that*. And when you see that, you see it's a great relief. That's all it is.

But then when you are firmly established in suchness—in that it's just this moment—you can begin again to play with the connections. Only, you've seen through them. So now they don't haunt you, because you know that there isn't any continuous "you," running on from moment to moment, who originated at some time in the past and will die at some time in the future. All that has disappeared. And you can have enormous fun anticipating the future, remembering the past, and playing all kinds of continuities. This is the meaning of that famous Zen saying about mountains are mountains:

> To the naive man, mountains are mountains, waters are waters. To the intermediate student, mountains are no longer

> mountains, waters are no longer waters. [In other words, they've all dissolved into the point-instant, to the *ksana*.] But for the fully perfected student, mountains are again mountains, and waters are again waters.

But there's a further elaboration to this, in which I can point out why it is not really necessary that the realization of the moment should destroy, let us simply call it, *the sense of life*. While it is true that there is only this point-instant—and that the spring does not become the summer—nevertheless, there are, in summer the traces of spring, and in winter the traces of summer. When you go down to the beach and you're on the sand and a bird was there sometime before you, the bird has left its tracks. Although the bird is not there, the tracks are, and you infer from the tracks that there *was* a bird. So in the same way, you infer from the plant that there was a seed, and just as the tracks are now on the sand, so the past is now in the memory.

In this sense, every *now* contains the past, and also contains the future. Every now is, therefore, at once a point-instant and a very rich universe full of everything. There is, therefore, no inconsistency—no incompatibility—between living totally in the present and also knowing and dealing with the past and the future. Except that, you see *there is no past*, and *will be no future*; they are extrapolations of the present—illusions manifested out of the present—*in* it, but not quite *of* it.

CHAPTER ELEVEN

FLOW AND MEDITATION I

This particular seminar is devoted to the subject of flow and its relation to meditation. And therefore, I have to talk to you first about certain characteristics of energy, because this world is energy ($E=mc^2$). And if there is nothing except energy, we cannot of course say what energy is because if everything is energy, then there is no class of events or things outside energy. And you can only describe something that you can put into a class—that is to say, something that you can put into an intellectual box. Although you can't describe energy—or you can't even describe reality—everybody knows perfectly well what it is. You simply feel it.

You feel energy in terms of a multiplicity of vibrations, and those vibrations can, of course, be measured—as we measure light, sound, heat, weight, and so forth. But we cannot experience all the vibrations of energy at the same time. That would be the same sort of confusion as if you slam down all the notes on the piano at once, or plucked all the strings of a harp at the same time. What we do, therefore, is we select. First of all, our senses are selective. The eye does not record the whole spectrum of light vibrations; the ear does not receive the whole spectrum of sound vibrations; they restrict themselves to a narrow band, and beyond that we select in various other ways.

There are certain vibrations which we consider noteworthy, important, and worth paying attention to, and others which we overlook as being insignificant and unimportant. A child will very often select experiences that adults deem ridiculous, because a child has not yet been taught how to select according to our preconceived notions of what should be picked out. So children will cherish rubbish, for example, which adults think should be thrown away. They will notice features of people's faces which are not supposed to be noticed—they will do all sorts of funny things like that.

And furthermore, a child will be taught which of these vibrations are "good" and which are "bad." The bad ones are, of course, to be avoided if possible. But inevitably they come up, because if you have a good-bad valuation of these various spectra, if you're going to have the good end of the spectrum, you also got to have the bad end. No matter how far you succeed in making life comfortable and pleasurable, you are looking at it with a scale. And at one end of the scale are the things called "good"; therefore, at the other end of the scale are the things called "bad." Now you may push the scale in the direction of good, you see, but there is always going to be a bad end—because there wouldn't be a good end if there weren't a bad end. Sometimes we feel the scale is going one way, and then we say things are getting worse and worse, because that's the way the scale is moving. But there's always the good end of it, so that when you're starving in a concentration camp, there are always certain events to which you look forward, and which sort of brighten things up.

You simply cannot have a continuous experience of life in which everything is completely bad or an experience of life in which everything is completely good. But we are under the illusion that this could be arranged, and it gives us a great deal of trouble being under that illusion. Anyhow, it makes sense. Indeed, in a very literal sense it makes sense that we should be selective. Just in the same way as when we play the piano or play the harp, we pick out all these vibrations in different orders, and that's the fun of it—that's the game of existence.

However, you can get hung up on your game. You can get into a fixed, rigid feeling that those vibrations which you were taught to select when you were a child—what people tell you—you can get hung up onto the idea that that way of selecting things is *the* way, and that there are not possible alternatives. Alternatively, you could get into a state of consciousness where you experience all vibrations simply as vibrations, and not deem them either good or bad. And that would be the point of view which Buddhists speak of as seeing the *suchness* of things. That is Zen: to dig whatever vibration happens, and feel it simply as something going *yoing, yoing, yoing, yoing, yoing, yoing, yoing*.

So then, when we are little babies we don't know how to interpret these vibrations. And when a baby cries, we assume it is reacting to the vibration called *pain*, or *discomfort*. The baby doesn't know at that point that that's a bad vibe; it just cries. And it doesn't know that crying is something you're not supposed to do. It's a perfectly natural reaction to the circumstance, but the adults don't like hearing babies cry. It makes them uncomfortable, because when they were babies they were taught that you're supposed to be uncomfortable when you cry. So as adults, they say, "Shut up!" and make the baby feel that crying is a bad thing. And if crying is a bad thing, then pain is a bad thing because there's no natural outlet afforded for the pain; and then, of course, the baby may get sick and run a fever.

A seventy-five-year-old man told me the other day that fever is one of the most exciting things in the world: it does all sorts of marvelous things to your consciousness. True, it does. But the baby is taught by the adult standing around its crib, wringing their hands, that the baby may die, that fever and sickness is a *bad* experience, and that the awful, awfuls is death. And so we learn to fear death, which is ridiculous, because death is as natural as birth; it isn't a form of sickness. But we've got this idea into our heads that we ought not to die—that under the most terrifying circumstances we are always to go on living. And therefore, we keep cancer patients intolerably suspended on the ends of tubes in hospitals, which are rather gloomy places, for endless amounts of time, just in the hope that a new cure for cancer might be discovered in the next week, or something miraculous. While there's life, there's hope. But hope is a rather questionable virtue because it indicates that life is always *going to come*, and isn't quite here.

Well, of course, as you should know, life, these vibrations, energy, are always present and never anywhere else. There are many different presents, of course, throughout the universe, because the universe is not here all at the same time. Certain stars or galaxies that we see today probably don't exist anymore, and certain ones that do exist are not yet seen—because the present is different everywhere. But nevertheless, there is no past, and there will be no future. There will only be a present. There always was a present. And you must see the past as *preceding from the present*, in the same way as the wake of a ship flows back from the prow, and then fades out. The wake doesn't drive the ship; the past does not create the present. But we are taught to think that it does. And we say we do what we do because we're motivated, because history requires it; it's the determination of the past, the destiny thing that brings about this. That's what Buddhists call *karma*. The object of Buddhism is liberation from karma, and you have to do that by straightening out your head.

But also, about death again—we are thoroughly indoctrinated into the idea that we have an instinct for survival, just as we have an instinct for reproduction and for eating. All this is nonsense based on Newtonian mechanics—that is to say, on a conception of the universe analogous to the game of billiards. The billiard balls are the atoms, celestial bodies, or what have you, and because they are hit by a cue they run around and bang each other about. And so, if we represent the individual ego as one of these billiard balls, you are supposed to do things only because you were hit by a cue—that is to say, because an instinct hit you, or a motivation, or an unconscious mental mechanism.

And you will realize, therefore, that psychoanalysis—and the whole philosophy of Freud—is really psycho-hydraulics: a discussion of psychological behavior by analogy with hydraulic systems, understood in terms of Newtonian mechanics. But that isn't necessarily the way things are; that is merely a *model* of the world, a kind of reconstruction. And as Alfred Korzybski never tired of pointing out, you must not "confuse the map with the territory."

There are many different ways, and many different models, which can be used for the behavior of the world. Now, we can't lay down one as the right model. But by using different models, we can see that there is no fixed model—that there are many ways of looking at life. I just gave you one; we normally think of the past *causing* the present, in the same way as if we set up a row of dominoes and we knock one down and the final one is knocked down by reason of all the others falling. That's our model of causality. But I also gave you the other one—of the ship, of the present making the past. You can look at it that way too. Now, I'm not trying to say which is the right one.

I'm going to show you that these are only your conceptions, which you plonk on the world—just in the same way that you interpret a Rorschach blot, because the world is something like a Rorschach blot; it is a wiggly patterning of energy. And the energy is the same as the patterning because there is no kind of stuff called "energy," which is formed into patterns, just as there is no kind of stuff called "matter," which is formed into things. The things (the shapes) are the matter. The word *matter* is the same as the word *meter*. Does it matter? Does it amount to anything? That is to say, is it solid? We say that something solid really amounts to something because you can't shove your finger through it—and it might shove itself through you. That matters; it measures up; it's important. But it isn't *made* of some kind of "stuff." Matter is simply an intense concentration of energy, and it always is on the move.

Everything is flux, like when you see a candle burning, and you say, "There is a flame." Now, a flame is a noun. But if I say, "The candle is burning," I am using a verb, and that is a little bit more accurate, I think, because the flame is a stream of hot gas, and it moves with tremendous rapidity. So there is no, as it were, gas permanently in the flame—it keeps running. But the shape stays for a while. In the same way, an eddy or whirlpool in water may stay constantly in the same place in a stream—for years—although, the water is passing through it all the time. But every time we come back and sit on that particular bank of the stream, we see the same old whirlpool.

Well, we are just the same as that. We are like flames, like whirlpools. And we are a stream—a very complex stream—consisting not only of electrical energy (which constitutes our nuclear shapes), but we are also a stream of water, milk, cereal, vegetables, beef steak, medicine, vitamins, heat, cosmic rays, and heaven only knows. All these things are pouring through us all the time. But we recognize each other because the way in which it's playing—the way in which this energy is dancing—keeps a fairly consistent form. We recognize those forms, and we say, "John Doe," "Mary Smith," etc.

But eventually, of course, it gives out—the form does what we call "get old." Although, we have ideas about that according to the way we've been brainwashed. We say, well, getting old isn't so good. But actually, it's very beautiful. You can completely readjust your thinking about this, and see old people as very lovely—even in their feebleness, in their slow motions, in hobbling around, leaning on a stick. If you get your head right, that's a very grand thing to do. I experienced this with my father, who grew to eighty-eight years old gracefully. And I've known many an old lady who were absolutely magnificent—and you know them too—because they completely accepted the process of aging, just as we accept the beautifully colored leaves in autumn. And as we say, we like a well-aged whiskey or a mature cheese—it's all the same kind of a thing. So we should understand that old people, for example, should be very much loved, and not call them "senior citizens," and put them away in some kind of a pokey place.

So then, if you've been brainwashed into certain fixed opinions all life long, there is some importance perhaps into becoming more flexible. Especially when a certain set of opinions that we call a "culture" (or a way of life) shows clear evidence of not working, or of crumbling. We are in that situation today, a situation where we see that the view of the universe which is fundamental to Western civilization—the Judeo-Christian picture of the world, even the nineteenth century materialistic picture of the world—these things are not working. People get terribly anxious when their basic view of how you should play the harp of life is not holding up; and therefore, under such circumstances we have to readjust our consciousness and reset, and find, perhaps, a new way of plucking the strings, or of structuring the world.

But in order to do that we have to pass through an intermediate state in which we learn to experience the vibrations without putting values on them—experiencing them without describing them, naming them, or trying to fit them into some system of concepts—good and bad, high class and low class, refined or crude, healthy or sick, or whatever. We have to write off all this sort of thing and learn to have what is called in Zen, *mushin*, meaning "no mind." That means not "no consciousness," but "no conceptions," "no fixed ideas," "no one-sided view of things." It's really easy to do that, but everybody wants to try and make it difficult.

People are compulsively complicated. So you might say that, in an inverse way, there is a certain difficulty in not becoming compulsively complicated. Because that requires a certain kind of intelligence: not what we call *intellectuality* in the ordinary way, not verbal intelligence—because that's not the only kind of intelligence. It requires *organic intelligence*—and that's the intelligence that you have in your organism that is responsible for your fantastically beautiful nervous system, for your veins, for your alimentary tract, for your glands, and for the color of your eyes.

But we are not ordinarily aware of being in any way responsible for that. That's something that seems to *happen to* us—just as, for example, we always think of gravity as something that just happens, and on the whole, is not a very good thing. In a way, humankind has been engaged in a struggle against gravity. For example, the beast goes on all fours, whereas human beings won't do that; they want to stand up and be on two legs; and they look at the bird with envy, and try to get up into the air—to conquer the sky—by force of some kind.

You know, in aeronautical theory we don't yet know how bees fly. Bees theoretically cannot fly, but they do. And the reason for the magnificent flight of birds and bees is that they're not fighting gravity—because, actually, everything in this universe is falling. The Earth is falling, but it falls in a circle. The Sun is falling, and it falls around some other star, way, way off. Every object is moving because it's falling, responding to gravity—and gravity is the nature of energy. Energy *is* gravity, because energy invariably takes the line of least resistance.

When you experience not taking the line of least resistance, you are not really using energy—you are using *force*—and force and energy are different. Force is the unintelligent use of energy; it is not following the easy course. And so when you force a key in a lock, you're liable to bend the key or break the lock—it does no good. Sometimes indeed, yes, we use strength.

There's a funny little old man some of you know, called Suzuki Roshi, who amazes very strong young men at his ability to move rocks. And they swear he moves them by leaning on them. It's uncanny what he does when he works in the garden at Tassajara. That's a kind of *judo*. And Zen very often involves the study of *judo*—*judo* meaning "the gentle way"—of finding out how the rock will respond to gravity, and helping it along those lines with your own gravity (your own weight). You use muscle very sparingly, but when you use your weight in the right place, that moves all sorts of things.

So one should in life—in all one's doings—have the sense that everything you do is falling. Even when you're climbing the stairs, you are falling up. Some people know this naturally, like babies, and people who haven't been taught proper posture and all that kind of thing. And many American Indians know this in a natural way, such that they don't make a noise when they walk. Whereas so many people, when they walk, they go thumping around so loudly you'd think there must be something wrong with them. Because if you walk like that in a forest, everything would either run away or run after you—they would know you were there—and in the forest you must be anonymous, you must be one with the forest. So it is said of the expert in Taoism:

Entering the forest,
  he does not disturb a blade of grass.
Entering the water,
  he doesn't make a ripple.

And you can watch some of those South Sea island swimmers dive: they seem to go into the water like a knife, making no splash. How's that done? When we dive, we jump on the end of the springboard, go zooming up, and then flip over in a jackknife way, and come down *SPLAT* with a great commotion all over the place. They just fall, and cut the water—so they are following the line of least resistance.

Now, the warning here, is very important. It is again to do with preconceptions. When we think of following the line of least resistance, what would it be like to do that? We have a notion in our minds that that would mean becoming droopy, improvident, feckless, or as we would say, behaving like an animal. Well now, animals are much better behaved than we are—much better. We are the world's greatest predators. Even sharks don't fly out of the water to eat us; they stay in the water. And if you really observe animal behavior, you will see that although they have fights and although they eat other things like we do, they are very, very orderly by and large in their behavior. And there are very few species of animals which practice torture on their own species. Very few.

But human beings are impossible. They are so fouled up by the confusion of their concepts with their organic life, with their religions, with their ideologies, with their this, that, and the other—over which they have the most appalling battles, which never can come to any reasonable outcome. Because you cannot, for example, arrange a compromise between black and white. Black and white are abstract conceptions. In nature there is no black and there is no white. There are *colors*, and both the black and the white worlds are discolored worlds.

So, getting back to the line of least resistance, Lao-tzu says of water, "Water seeks the low level, which men abhor. Nothing in the world is weaker than water, and yet, it can overcome the hardest things." When you watch water flowing over dry ground, you see it moving along and then it suddenly puts out a lot of fingers, and then only one of those fingers continues—because it's feeling out the path—and it gradually goes down and down, and if it gets into a place where it forms into a pool, it waits there. And then it rises, and finds a place where it can go over, and it goes on. So the use of energy is the same.

And that, then, is a secret in the art of meditation—which means that you don't force things, you don't *try* to meditate. Now *meditation* is a bad English word for what they do in yoga and in Zen. They don't meditate, because whenever you say to an Easterner who practices meditation, "What do you meditate *on*?" they look vaguely puzzled, and say, "Well, we just meditate. We don't meditate on something." Because what meditation consists of, essentially, is *being aware without conceptualizing*. In other words, learning to get rid of the verbal chatter that goes on constantly inside one's head—what I call "thinking"—and temporarily stopping that. It isn't that thinking is bad; it's only that thinking *all the time* is bad. That would be like talking all the time, and never listening to anyone else.

So the problem for many people is how to stop thinking, because it's become a habit. It's a nervous tic to think all the time, and so we create endless problems by doing this. For example, people who have various miseries lie awake nights thinking about them; they chatter to themselves over and over and over and over and over again, about their problems, and don't know how to stop it. So in the course of this weekend, we are going to explore experimentally, various ways of enabling our awareness (or our minds) to be quiet.

You know, Tim Leary made the famous remark that "to come to your senses, you must go out of your mind," where *mind* means certain fixed thought patterns, certain fixed valuations of how one ought to select experience. And Ronald Laing, in his book, *The Politics of Experience*, has pointed out that we have an etiquette concerning what experiences are legitimate in just the same way that we have an etiquette as to what gestures are legitimate. You know, you're not supposed to put out your tongue at people—except in Tibet, where it's a remark of respect. You're not supposed to be what they call *an exhibitionist*. You are not supposed to do all sorts of things that are taboo gestures.

Well, in exactly the same way, there are taboo experiences which you really aren't allowed to have, and if you start having taboo experiences, they're going to put you in the nuthouse. They're going to call you a schizophrenic, a psychotic, a paranoid, a psychopath, and all sorts of bad names, because, you see, these are the new up-to-date forms of heresy. And just as the heresy was a taboo form of religious belief at one time, nobody takes religion seriously today; we don't have the Inquisition anymore. The not having an Inquisition is a function of not taking religion seriously, and I mean, in the kind of religion in which you have heaven and hell. If we did take it seriously we'd still have an Inquisition because we would think it was terribly important that we saved people from going to hell.

But today, what we take seriously is people's psychiatric state. So you can, in other words, be imprisoned without due process of law, confined under unspeakable circumstances, and literally tortured for your own good—just as Inquisitors of the Catholic Church tortured heretics for their own good. It's the same old thing, all over again. Only it keeps changing its place in the spectrum, so that we suddenly are unaware where we are doing things like that.

So we are watching the beginnings of a psychiatric revolution, represented by people like Thomas Szasz and Ronald Laing, to break up what they call *psychiatric fascism*, and to ask for due rights for the so-called "insane"—just as earlier in history, the Protestants and religious libertarians were asking for due rights for freedom of religion.

We will need a new Magna Carta for freedom of consciousness, and of course, all the brouhaha going on about psychedelic chemicals, and marijuana, and so on, is a religious fight. It's all the same kind of thing as the quarrels that we had in the past over sacraments. Who had the true sacrament, whether this Catholic formula was the right way of transforming the sacrament, or whether the Protestant formula wasn't just as good, and all that kind of thing. It's all happening all over again, and it's just wonderful to see the repetitious patterns in humanity's history. It's sometimes rather depressing too.

So then, in meditation, the real art of it is to be free from concepts. But that implies something else very difficult for Americans to understand: that you are not meditating when you are meditating for a purpose, or when you are doing it because you think it's good for you, because you think you are going to improve yourself. But you can't improve yourself—or anybody else, for that matter—just as you can't lift yourself up by your own bootstraps. And when you give up trying to improve yourself, you have all that energy available for things that can actually be done.

So when there is no thought about self-improvement, about going somewhere, about achieving a different state of consciousness, then you are simply being *here*. That's the only place you can be, actually. Because when you remember the past, your memories are present experiences; when you anticipate the future, your anticipations are present experiences. There is nowhere else to be. Where's your hurry?

So the art of meditation is, essentially, relaxing the verbal commentary on the world that constantly goes on, and coming to center, which is the present—or coming to center in the sense that gravity teaches you to center yourself.

CHAPTER TWELVE

FLOW AND MEDITATION II

So then, I was talking to you this morning about the dynamics of energy, about the way in which we select vibrations, and about the basic principles of meditation as a process for bringing about mental quiet, as it is understood in yoga, Buddhism, and Zen.

Silence of the mind is not pure passivity or mental limpness, just as physical relaxation is not physical limpness—as if you were a wet rag hung over a clothesline. In the process of meditation one is completely aware of all sensory inputs. You don't try to shut off your senses, and although it may be helpful to begin in meditation by closing the eyes, in the Zen philosophy of meditation you don't close your eyes. If you do, you're called a "denizen of the dark cavern." Instead you look at the floor about four feet in front of you, and you allow the light to play with your eyes without putting any names on these patterns of light and shade and color, just as you allow the sound waves in the air to play with your ears. But you don't put any name upon it; you allow yourself to be in a non-conceptual way.

Now, the importance of this is the practical effect—although, when you are in meditation, you are not concerned with practical effects.

Practical effects accrue as a byproduct, just as happiness—which cannot be pursued—is a byproduct of being interested in something else. But the disease of civilization is that we confuse the world of symbols with the world of reality. As I said this morning, you all know what reality is, and it doesn't have to be explained to you. If you try to define it, you become a professional philosopher, and you will eventually shrivel up and die—but all the while you know what it is.

We are in a very serious condition in the world today because of the confusion of symbolic reality with real reality. We are trying to make as the goals of life the attainment of pleasures that really exist as symbols only—and the chief example of this is lots of money. There are no limits to the amount of money you can make if you are sufficiently clever and sufficiently ruthless—you can go on and on and on and on. But there are very strict limits to the amount of beef you can eat at one meal, to the number of houses you can live in, to the amount of clothes you can wear.

Supposing you wore three suits or dresses a day and you wanted to be different all the time—all right, there are 365 days of the year, multiply that by three, and that's enough suits for anyone. Also, there is a practical limit. If you were wearing a completely different suit for one third of the day, and you never wore it again, after a while that would become a bit absurd. You might find a favorite suit, one that you felt suited you—what is a suit, except something *that suits you*—and you would go back to it, and you would want that one again. You can have hundreds of houses if you're very rich, but you find you have a favorite one and you want to go back to it. So there are limits to what we can enjoy in a material, physical, real sense.

Although I must say when I say *real*—and I also join with that the words *physical* and *material*—the real world is not necessarily physical or material. The ideas that come out of the history of Western culture, that we say "physical" or "material," these are purely conceptual. When somebody says, "I'm a materialist, and I think there is nothing but material, and all this spiritual stuff is just fantasy," the idea of material is itself fantasy. These flowers are not material. Material is an idea; it's a concept. These flowers, you can only understand by looking at them and feeling them; we don't know what they are. We see the patterns of energy, and the delight of them.

But a person who says, "Well, this is just material" does not realize that they're some kind of a fantast. They're trying to put their personality up against the spiritual people, who say, "The real thing in life is beyond all these things that we see and hear," and so on, "there is a happy land far, far away"—you know, there is some kind of a thing beyond all this, and that is a kind of spiritual one-upmanship. People in religion are the worst game players in the world; they're always trying to out-face each other, and say, "Well, you don't have quite the right conception."

Even among the most orthodox confraternities of, say, orthodox Catholic theologians, they're always trying to one-up each other, and say, "Yes, you believe that your explanation of the doctrine of the Trinity is very correct, but there are certain subtle respects in which you haven't quite got the point." And they go round and round and round on this forever, because it's not really religion at all; it's a form of personal contest, and nearly everybody in the world is challenging someone else to say, "You're not real, are you? You're not really sincere. You don't actually mean what you say. Do you love me? Do you really love me? Prove it. I don't think you can."

So everybody is frightened, everybody feels guilty, and everybody knows how to exploit everybody else's fear and guilt. And emotions like guilt are absolutely useless because they always frustrate their own objective. Guilt is supposed to make you good, but it's like alcoholism, where the more terrible an alcoholic feels about their dependence on alcohol, the more they drink. The same with jealousy. If I am jealous of the woman I love, terribly jealous, and won't allow her to have any other male friends, she hates me all the more for being jealous of her. I can't keep a woman by being jealous of her, and she can't keep me by the inverse process. So all those emotions deny themselves.

We have to see that all these are games of spiritual one-upmanship, and we have to see through them. Every guru or spiritual teacher comes on like they've got something that you don't have: more insight, more relaxation, more happiness, more oneness with God—whatever it may be. And this is the bait, which they use to catch you. Now there are two kinds of gurus; one kind of guru really believes he's got more than you have, and he can do nothing for you except lead you into a closed bag. That's the ordinary minister, who believes that he is the representative of the true and authentic religion, and that he's going to get you into the church and he's going to get you hooked on the religion, so that you become a religious addict. And so, of course, so long as you're a religious addict, just like a drug addict you will have to fork out fifty bucks a day to get his connection. So you're going to have to tithe your income to help pay off the mortgage on the church building and to keep the clergy alive—and that's why they want to get you hooked on it.

There's another kind of guru, and he makes his living in an entirely different way. He wants to get rid of you. He's got some way of liberating you so that you can function on your own without having any guru at all, and without belonging to any religion—because he treats his doctrine, his practice, as a medicine not as a diet. And eventually you take the medicine and you understand, you can function on your own, and you go away. But when you go away, you say, "Hey!" to everybody else, "I got this guru, he was just fabulous, and he set me free." So this kind of guru, instead of having a permanent group of followers, has a big turnover, and he gets on alright. So here I'm just explaining the economics of spirituality.

And there is another side to this, incidentally. Wherever a guru happens to liberate people instead of enslaving them, other people will want to do the same thing—and that's all right. If you are a closed-type guru—where you want people to stick around to pay the mortgage—you don't want any other gurus in competition with you, because that's taking away business. I had a very funny adventure in Thailand related to this. With my gaze cast downward, I was wandering around a temple, and suddenly came across a bookstall, and there was a book on the kind of meditation they do in Southern Buddhism. So just sort of talking out loud to myself, I said, "Oh! That must be *satipatthana*."

And a voice said, "You practice *satipatthana*?"

I looked up and there was a yellow-robed monk, who spoke English, standing in charge of the bookstall. He was kind of red-eyed, and I looked at him and said, "Well, not exactly. I practice Zen."

"Oh, Zen not *satipatthana*."

"Well," I said, "it's all kind of the same thing. It's like yoga."

"No, no! *Satipatthana* not yoke."

"Now listen," I said, "you Buddhists are supposed to be open-minded, and to believe that there are many, many ways of realization."

"No. *Satipatthana* only correct way."

"Well," I said, "you talk like a Roman Catholic. They say they have the only true way; you say you have the only true way." I said, "You know what you're like, you've got a ferryboat concession to ferry people across the river, and a few miles down the river somebody else opens up a ferryboat, and you complain to the police and the government saying, 'He shouldn't open up because he's in competition with me.'"

Now, when it comes to the economics of spirituality, the truth of the matter is this: in London, there was a street called Harley Street, where every eminent physician and surgeon wanted to have an office. And so Harley Street became completely full with physicians and surgeons. You would think, naturally, they were all in competition with each other. But nothing of the kind happened, and they all became equally prosperous, so that they had to open up Wimpole Street, which was next to Harley Street, and it filled up with physicians and surgeons. And when they had filled that street up, they opened up Welbeck Street, which ran along next to it. And when they filled that up, they got Queen Anne's Street, which ran parallel. The whole area became nothing but physicians, surgeons and dentists, and they were all fantastically prosperous because they had the right address. Once you got into Harley Street, you were there.

And likewise, if you're a guru and you set up in Sausalito or Big Sur or Hollywood you're in the right place. We can take any number, and the more we have, the more prosperous everybody will be. This is *the economics of plenty*, and if you really work it right, it's all based on a big turnover. You don't try to capture people. You don't try to make them faithful to you, don't want to tie them up. But if you set them all free, you really get them going. That's what you're supposed to do, that's your job—to liberate them—and then they're grateful, and send their friends to you.

So, this is the craft of mysticism—and I just want to be very frank with you, because after all, you pay to come to these seminars. But in India it is considered very immoral to ask for money for spiritual teaching, but that's a different culture from our own. In the United States it would be immoral *not* to ask for money, because in the United States people disrespect anything they get free, and they have to give money as a token of their sincerity. Just as in India or in China you have to give something else: you have to wait a long time; you have to be persistent in token of your sincerity. But in this country, the hang up is money, so naturally, one asks for money. A person like myself only needs a relatively small amount of money, and so if you make an awful lot of it by being a successful guru, you give the rest away, or do something creative and imaginative with it. Allen Ginsberg has a foundation; he makes a great deal of money by being a crazy poet, and he gives all that he doesn't need to help other poets.

So then, the point I'm making is this: I explained to you this morning that if you really meditate, you come into the pure present. But you are not trying to gain anything, to alter your state of mind from what it is now into some other state which you think it *ought* to be in; you are centering in *where you are*. But the difficulty for us with this is that we do everything—we even eat, we play, we dance—under the fundamental assumption that all this is good for us. We go to concerts to improve our culture, to the theater, to the movie in order to be able to say we have become more educated, we have improved. And as a result of this kind of motivation, we don't really do those things at all. If you go to the concert to become more cultured, you are not really listening.

So meditation above all things—because it's got a slightly disciplinary flavor to it, a slightly religious flavor to it—is something that people use to somehow get ahead in the game of spiritual one-upmanship. And I get sick and tired of people who go and study Zen, and come back and brag about the long hours of meditation they put in, and how much their legs hurt, and what a great ordeal it was, and how good it was for them, and how you who have not gone through this discipline are a kind of underling. I've had this put on me for years, because I didn't go to Japan and didn't sit around in Zendos—but just worked it my own way. And they say, "Well, you are just a dilettante.

You haven't suffered as much as we have, and you really ought to suffer. You ought to put up with those long, long endurance tests."

Now the reason why, in meditation, one sits in a certain way—whether you sit like I'm sitting now on my knees, or whether you sit in the lotus posture—is that your legs become a little uncomfortable. And the reason for that is not self-punitive; it's merely that it helps you to stay awake—that's all. It's like if you were floating in a hot tub with supports in a completely dark room—perhaps in one of those sensory deprivation chambers—you would very likely go to sleep. But the point in meditation is to be wide awake—very wide awake—without, however, the intellectual chatter going on in the head. And so a posture that involves a very certain subordinate degree of discomfort keeps you awake. Actually, when you get used to sitting this way, it becomes natural.

But as I explained, the point is to be wide, wide awake and aware of your total sensory input without confusing it with the symbolic world of words and concepts—so that you experience life naked and directly, and experience *you* naked and directly without having in your head the concept of who you are as a role player, as a personality, as an ego. And this becomes, in due course, a very pleasant thing to do, so that meditation becomes not something that you put in so much time at—like you might put in time in a jail—but it becomes a pleasure.

Of course, from the point of view of our religion in the United States that is almost sinful. Religion is not supposed to be a pleasure, because it's supposed to be joining with Christ in suffering on the cross. But there is enough inevitable suffering going on anyhow, enough suffering to supply anybody's masochistic needs. You are going to die one of these days. Everybody encounters difficulties in their lives; you don't need to go out of your way to seek them.

Now, there are two fundamental approaches to meditation. The first we experimented with this morning, when Charlotte Selver was getting us to bounce on our heels, and to stretch as tightly as we could to overcome gravity, and then after that, she said, "See what happens when you don't do it." So one of the methods of meditation is to stretch as tightly as possible—to concentrate with your whole energy on a point, and to use the maximum amount of effort. In yoga, there is an exercise called *kumbhaka*, which is a way of breathing rather forcefully, holding the breath as long and as tightly as you can—that's like the stretching we did. That's like those people in the Tendai temple up on Mt. Hiei, over Kyoto, who practice thousands and thousands of bowings: they stand up, they kneel down, and prostrate themselves on the floor, stand up again, kneel down, prostrate themselves on the floor.

And there are those Tibetan monks who do the *lung-gom-pa*; they run through the mountain trails with enormous leaps—like the dancer Nijinsky, who could do those enormous leaps where you pause a little bit in the air and seem to overcome gravity, and then drop again—and they go on and on and on, bouncing along the road. Or there are other pilgrims that prostrate themselves at every step while traveling a long journey. There are people who run the streets of Kyoto, a hundred miles every day, at a jog trot. There are all kinds of things like that where you work yourself to a limit, and as a result, struggle.

Because in doing that you get a thing which runners call "second wind." And second wind in running is where *you* are no longer running, but it *runs you*. Where, in other words, the ego energy in the running is displaced and the energy of the whole organism takes over. And that is the energy of the whole universe—when you get second wind. So you get second wind in this fierce kind of meditation practice.

Alternatively, there is another way in; and this way is a kind of so-called "easy way," and one uses it for a different type of personality. There are certain people who must have the difficult way because they don't know they exist unless they are sitting on a spike. And those kind of people, who don't believe they are real unless they hurt, have to follow the difficult way. But there is a subtle way, which is a Taoistic approach, wherein, instead of trying to master and dominate your body-mind, you let go of it—and you let it do whatever it wants to do.

Let's suppose for a moment, for the sake of example, that you just close your eyes and allow your eardrums to respond to any sound going on. There are no proper sounds or improper sounds. You may feel free to shift, shuffle, cough, sneeze as you will. Don't try to identify, locate, or name the sounds that you hear, just let the rippling air play with your eardrums. And as you hear the sound of my voice coming across to you, listen to what I have to say simply as tones. Your brain will take care of understanding it; you don't try to understand.

In other words, allow your ears to hear anything they want to hear. And to assist you in this, keep your tongues relaxed, floating easily in the lower jaw. Listen to every sound in the whole field of air vibrations as you would listen to music, as you would listen to Bach or Ravi Shankar—without trying to see any meaning in it. And remember to keep the tongue relaxed—there is no hurry. You're not going anywhere; you are always *here*. This is *what there is*.

And of course, one can do that through all the senses—not just the ears, but the body feeling, the skin contact, the breath, the sense of smell, taste, and also of course, the eyes. It's more difficult to do this with the eyes, because as Marshall McLuhan pointed out in his book *The Gutenberg Galaxy*, our culture is excessively visual. Because of making sense out of print and the enormous valuation placed on literacy, we have over-balanced one sense—the visual sense—and somehow need to restore that balance to all the senses.

And well, of course, we have undervalued smell. When we say to somebody, "you smell," that's uncomplimentary. We should say, correctly, "you stink," if we mean you have a bad smell. But everything connected with smell is repressed; and therefore, because we still continue to smell, it is an unconscious sense through which we relate to each other in ways that we don't know. You take an instinctive liking to someone because you like the smell, but you don't know that. You take an instinctive dislike to someone because you don't like the smell, but you don't know that. All sorts of things, all sorts of messages are passed through the nose, but often we are not aware of them. We do not have an adequate vocabulary of smell. Only three adjectives in English are associated with smell uniquely: *acrid*, *pungent*, *fragrant*. All the others are associated with, or borrowed from, other senses. Think how many adjectives we have for vision, for sound, for taste—although taste, of course, is inseparable from smell.

This is the second way of meditation, which I was demonstrating to you by your hearing, allowing your ears to hear whatever they want to hear. In the same way, you allow your breath to breathe any way it wants to breathe. You allow your muscle skin feeling, the sense of touch, to feel any way it wants to feel. You allow your eyes to see anything they want to see. And finally, you allow your mind to think anything it wants to think—let it go. This is the relaxed way. The other way is the tense way. They come to the same conclusion. You go around this way, take the right-hand path and go there, or take the left-hand path and go there.

So you might say the right-hand path is the tough way; the left-hand path is the easy, relaxed way. One is the path of the straight man, the other is the path of the cunning man. I'm not going to evaluate between one and the other. It's up to the individual to take the way they want to take. But the way Charlotte and I have been interested in for a long time is the way which is natural—which doesn't force things—and which lets the organism with its own inner sense of what is correct do it by itself. That is following the line of least resistance—that's the left-hand path.

So, if you will leave your mind alone, you don't try to concentrate it, you don't try to discipline it. You merely let it do whatever it wants to do. Whatever thoughts want to flow through your head, let them flow. Don't try either to get with them and make something of it, and don't try to stop them. Just let them go. Besides, *who are you* as distinct from your thoughts, as distinct from your visual, auditory, tactile, olfactory sensations? Who might intervene, and say, you do otherwise?

Because when we get that terrific split between our *experience*, our feelings, our sensations on the one hand, and on the other something called *the experiencer*—the control agent who has and who directs all these things—there's the root of our trouble. Because we are confusing ourselves with an image of ourselves, which is not the living organism. And under those circumstances, we define the living organism as a material object—the body which corrupts, and which is somehow antithetical to spirit—not realizing that the idea of the body as something antithetical to spirit is purely a conception. When I clap my hands, like this, it is not a conception. As we see it now from the standpoint of twentieth century quantum physics, it's a shimmering phenomenon of electrical energy—it's a light show. This isn't what we used to think of as physical at all, you know, that blocky chunky stuff. It's a sizzing dance—it's like fire.

That's the meaning of the Buddhist figure Fudo, this guy with a sword in one hand and a rope in the other, with a fierce face and flames all around him. *Fudo* means "immovable." He's showing you everything is fire. It's like I said this morning, a flame seems to be "a flame"—a thing that sticks in one position—but it's nothing of the kind. So Fudo, this flaming God with a sword which cuts off all entanglements, he cuts loose our conceptions so that we can see this all-too-solid flesh dissolve, and find ourselves flowing.

FLOW AND MEDITATION II

Notes

Editor's Preface

1. Al Chung-liang Huang, Foreword, *Tao: The Watercourse Way* (New York: Pantheon, 1975), p. x.

2. Alan Watts, *Tao: The Watercourse Way* (New York: Pantheon, 1975), p. xiv.

3. Huang, op. cit., p. ix.

4. Watts, op. cit., p. 17.

Chapter Seven

1. See Herbert A. Giles, ed. and trans., *Chuang-tzu: Mystic, Moralist, and Social Reformer* (Shanghai: Kelly and Walsh, 1926) for all references to the Chuang-tzu.

2. See Lin Yutang, ed. and trans., *The Wisdom of Lao-tse* (New York: Modern Library, 1948).

About Alan Watts

Born on January 6, 1915 in Chislehurst, England, Alan Watts was an influential interpreter of Eastern wisdom traditions for Western audiences. As a prolific writer and speaker, Watts brought Buddhist, Taoist, and Hindu philosophies to life, making them widely accessible and revealing their essential relevance to modern culture. Endlessly intrigued with the questions of human identity and spiritual awakening, his work spanned the realms of religion, philosophy, psychology, ecology, and mysticism.

At the young age of 15, Watts immersed himself in the study of Zen and Vedanta at the Buddhist Lodge in London. After meeting and being deeply influenced by the Zen scholar-practitioner D.T. Suzuki, Watts published his first book, *The Spirit of Zen*, in 1936 at the age of 21, before moving to New York, where he continued to write and practice Zen. Soon thereafter, Watts turned back to Western religion, earning a master's degree in theology from Seabury-Western Theological Seminary in Evanston, Illinois. His thesis was published as *Behold the Spirit: A Study in the Necessity of Mystical Religion*, and he became an Episcopal chaplain at Northwestern University.

In 1950, Watts left the Church, and moved back to New York, where he spent time with Joseph Campbell and John Cage. In the spring of 1951, he departed to the West Coast to teach Buddhism at the American Academy of Asian Studies in San Francisco. Drawing quite a crowd, his classes at the Academy blossomed into evening lectures open to the public, and spilled over to local coffee houses frequented by Beat poets and writers. Once established in the Bay Area, Watts began the radio show "Way Beyond the West" at station

KPFA, which rapidly gained popularity, as did his public TV program "Eastern Wisdom and Modern Life." Watts wrote numerous books during this period, including *The Wisdom of Insecurity*, *The Way of Zen*, *Psychotherapy East and West*, and *The Book: On the Taboo Against Knowing Who You Are*, all of which helped solidify his stature as a luminary of the 1960s counterculture.

By the late 1960s, Watts was adopted as a spiritual spokesperson by a generation of truth-seekers, and he lived on a ferryboat in Sausalito in a waterfront community of bohemians, artists, and other cultural renegades. His ferryboat, the SS Vallejo, soon became such a popular destination that to maintain his focus on writing, he moved into a cabin on the nearby slopes of Mount Tamalpais. There he became part of the Druid Heights artist community. Continuing to travel on lecture tours into the early 1970s, Watts was increasingly drawn to life on the mountain, where he wrote his mountain journals (later published as *Cloud Hidden, Whereabouts Unknown*), penned his monograph *The Art of Contemplation*, worked on his autobiography *In My Own Way*, and wrote the first five chapters of his final book, *Tao: The Watercourse Way*.

After returning from a whirlwind lecture tour that took him through the U.S., Canada, and Europe, Watts passed away peacefully in his sleep on November 16, 1973, on the mountain he loved. Throughout his life, Watts wrote 23 major books and conducted several hundred seminars and lectures, many of which were recorded and are now maintained by the Alan Watts Organization.

Also by Alan Watts

The Spirit of Zen (1936)
The Legacy of Asia and Western Man (1937)
The Meaning of Happiness (1940)
Behold the Spirit (1948)
Easter: Its Story and Meaning (1950)
The Supreme Identity (1950)
The Wisdom of Insecurity (1951)
Myth and Ritual in Christianity (1953)
The Way of Zen (1957)
Nature, Man, and Woman (1958)
Beat Zen, Square Zen, and Zen (1959)
This Is It: And Other Essays on Zen and Spiritual Experience (1960)
Psychotherapy East and West (1961)
The Joyous Cosmology: Adventures in the Chemistry of Consciousness (1962)
The Two Hands of God: The Myths of Polarity (1963)
Beyond Theology: The Art of Godmanship (1964)
The Book: On the Taboo Against Knowing Who You Are (1966)
Nonsense (1967)
Does it Matter? Essays on Man's Relation to Materiality (1970)
Erotic Spirituality: The Vision of Konarak (1971)
In My Own Way: An Autobiography (1972)
The Art of Contemplation (1972)
Cloud-Hidden, Whereabouts Unknown (1973)
Tao: The Watercourse Way (1975)

Posthumous Books

The Essence of Alan Watts (1975)

Uncarved Block, Unbleached Silk (1978)

Om: Creative Meditations (1979)

Play to Live (1982)

The Way of Liberation (1983)

The Essential Alan Watts (1984)

Out of the Trap (1985)

Diamond Web (1986)

The Early Writings of Alan Watts (1987)

The Modern Mystic: A New Collection of Early Writings (1990)

Talking Zen (1994)

Become What You Are (1995)

Buddhism: The Religion of No-Religion (1995)

The Philosophies of Asia (1995)

The Tao of Philosophy (1995)

Myth and Religion (1996)

Seeds of Genius: The Early Writings of Alan Watts (1997)

Taoism: Way Beyond Seeking (1997)

Zen and the Beat Way (1997)

The Culture of Counter-Culture (1998)

Eastern Wisdom: Three Classics in One Volume (2000)

Still the Mind: An Introduction to Meditation (2000)

What is Tao? (2000)

What is Zen? (2000)

Zen, The Supreme Experience (2002)

Eastern Wisdom, Modern Life: Collected Talks, 1960–1969 (2006)
Out of Your Mind (2017)
Alan Watts—In the Academy: Essays and Lectures (2017)
The Collected Letters of Alan Watts (2017)
Just So: Money, Materialism, and the Ineffable, Intelligent Universe (2020)
The Fish Who Found the Sea (2020)
There Is Never Anything But the Present (2021)
Wandering Nowhere (2023)

In addition to his printed works, Alan Watts recorded hundreds of lectures and seminars, including the sessions on Taoism upon which this book is based. For a complete listing of available recorded talks, please visit www.AlanWatts.org. There you will also discover an extended list of his written works, including popular and academic articles he published, as well as a multitude of books and articles written about his life and works.

About the Editors

Mark Watts is the son of renowned spiritual teacher Alan Watts, and the Director and Founder of the Alan Watts Organization, which is dedicated to the preservation and creative dissemination of Alan Watts' audio-video legacy. Starting in 1968, Mark recorded hundreds of his father's talks, and in 1973, co-founded the Electronic University, precursor to the Alan Watts Organization. Over the years he has curated and produced the talks for public radio and dozens of collaborative media projects. Mark also produced the Joseph Campbell Audio Collection, and created archival projects for the San Francisco Zen Center and Plum Village. In addition to AV production, Mark oversees licensing and outreach efforts, and is host of the Alan Watts podcast "Being in the Way."

Dr. Brian Wheeler is an Alan Watts scholar, freelance editor and writer, and student of the human condition. He holds a PhD in East-West Psychology and an MA in Philosophy and Religion, both from the California Institute of Integral Studies (CIIS) in San Francisco, California. Upon learning that, in the 1950s, Alan Watts was a professor and dean at the American Academy of Asian Studies—now known as CIIS—he spent a decade of study and research at the university, exploring human nature and Watts' body of writings and lectures. Dr. Wheeler wrote his dissertation on "Paradox and the Cosmology of Alan Watts," portions of which have been published in the *Journal of Humanistic Psychology*. He serves as the Resident Scholar at the Alan Watts Organization, and has a deep interest in human potential, yoga, tea, and the tantric wisdom traditions of India and Tibet.

Made in the USA
Columbia, SC
19 August 2024